MASTERING
MUAY THAI
KICK-BOXING

D1601897

MASTERING
MUAY THAI
KICK-BOXING

**MMA-Proven
Techniques**

JOE E. HARVEY

TUTTLE PUBLISHING
Tokyo • Rutland, Vermont • Singapore

CREDITS

Foreword by Patrick T. Tray **Submissions Advisor** Jeff Johnston

Models and Photo Credits

Rick Tavares: Green/Camo Ana Saldana: Pink
Michael Custodio: Blue Richard S. Hemsley: Red/Black
James W. Imel: Black (Fig. 160–166) Scott Harlan: Olive Green (Fig. 112, 113, 122, and 123)
Combination and Endurance Drills Courtesy of Trident Academy of Martial Arts

---

Disclaimer: Please note that the publisher and author of this instructional book are NOT RESPONSIBLE in any manner whatsoever for any injury that may result from practicing the techniques and/or following the instructions given within. Martial arts training can be dangerous—both to you and to others—if not practiced safely. If you're in doubt as to how to proceed or whether your practice is safe, consult with a trained martial arts teacher before beginning. Since the physical activities described herein may be too strenuous in nature for some readers, it is also essential that a physician be consulted prior to training.

Published by Tuttle Publishing, an imprint of Periplus Editions (HK) Ltd., with editorial offices at 364 Innovation Drive, North Clarendon, Vermont 05759 U.S.A.

Copyright © 2009 Joe E. Harvey

All rights reserved. No part of this publication may be reproduced or utilized in any form or by any means, electronic or mechanical, including photocopying, recording, or by any information storage and retrieval system, without prior written permission from the publisher.

Harvey, Joe E.
   Mastering Muay Thai kick-boxing : MMA-proven techniques / Joe E. Harvey. -- 1st ed.
      p. cm.
   ISBN 978-0-8048-4005-7 (pbk.)
   1. Muay Thai. I. Title.
   GV1127.T45H37 2009
   796.815--dc22

                         2008053312

DISTRIBUTED BY

North America,
Latin America & Europe
Tuttle Publishing
364 Innovation Drive
North Clarendon
VT 05759-9436 U.S.A.
Tel: 1 (802) 773-8930
Fax: 1 (802) 773-6993
info@tuttlepublishing.com
www.tuttlepublishing.com

Japan
Tuttle Publishing
Yaekari Building, 3rd Floor
5-4-12 Osaki
Shinagawa-ku
Tokyo 141 0032
Tel: (81) 3 5437-0171
Fax: (81) 3 5437-0755
tuttle-sales@gol.com

Asia Pacific
Berkeley Books Pte. Ltd.
61 Tai Seng Avenue #02-12
Singapore 534167
Tel: (65) 6280-1330
Fax: (65) 6280-6290
inquiries@periplus.com.sg
www.periplus.com

First edition
12 11 10 09   6 5 4 3 2 1

Printed in Singapore

TUTTLE PUBLISHING® is a registered trademark of Tuttle Publishing, a division of Periplus Editions (HK) Ltd.

Previous page: The straight knee #2 is a defense against an opponent's right cross and includes a follow-up strike. Learn more about this technique on page 86.

Opposite: The left head pull is a defense against an opponent's right skip knee or right curve knee in the plum/clinch. Learn more about this technique on page 155.

DEDICATION

To Richard Ernest Harvey
A true warrior

CONTENTS

*Are included in description of another technique.

FOREWORD

Muay Thai is a ring fighting art and the national sport of Thailand. Its roots come from the combative and ancient art of Krabi Krabong. Some refer to it as Thailand's weapon art; however, it was more than just an art: it was the way the Thai's fought wars. The techniques utilized in Krabi Krabong easily transferred over to the techniques used early on in the sport of Muay Thai, which has evolved over time to its current stature in the world of martial arts and international sports.

Muay Thai is one of the fastest growing fight sports in the world. Due to its popularity and effectiveness in the ring, it has become one of the most prominent arts in the Mixed Martial Arts (MMA) arena. Muay Thai's effectiveness in the ring and MMA has become common knowledge to fans and fighters throughout the world.

What is not common knowledge is the effectiveness and widespread use of Muay Thai in the military. I spent over 21 years with the U.S. Navy SEAL Teams and throughout that time, I witnessed numerous hand-to-hand combat programs that were designed to market and teach military and law enforcement. If it is a successful program, you can bet that Muay Thai plays a large role in it. At my school, the Trident Academy of Martial Arts, we teach numerous martial arts, including Muay Thai, in a program that combines the most practical techniques for self-defense from all the arts taught. Muay Thai is the most prominent art in that program for two reasons: 1) the effectiveness of Muay Thai technique and 2) the training method of Muay Thai.

Joe Harvey is a practitioner of numerous arts; however, at my academy, he was a student of Muay Thai. When I refer to Joe as a student of Muay Thai, I am not referring to him as someone who only trained in it, but as someone who studied the art intensely. He meticulously took notes, became well-versed in the art and thoroughly understood all the techniques and training methods. After viewing his notes, which are the foundation of this book, I cannot recommend a better representation of Muay Thai than that found within these pages. It is an outstanding aid to anybody training in Muay Thai or MMA. Joe's instructions are easy to follow, they break down the techniques in detail for both beginners and advanced students and put together intricate combinations. I highly recommend this book to all interested in Muay Thai or MMA.

—Patrick Tray

Patrick Tray is a four-time combat veteran who served 21 years as a member of the U.S. Navy SEAL Teams and served as the SEAL's hand-to-hand combat instructor for over 10 years. Mr. Tray, owner and founder of Trident Academy of Martial Arts, is a full instructor and representative for the Thai Boxing Association of the U.S.A. (TBA-USA) and has full instructorship in Jun Fan Gung Fu/Jeet Kune Do Concepts and Filipino martial arts under Dan Inosanto. He is also a full instructor and representative for other martial arts (e.g., Brazilian Jiu-Jitsu, combat submission wrestling—CSW) under world-renowned instructors.

INTRODUCTION

MUAY THAI

Interest in the art of Muay Thai is rapidly growing worldwide due to its practical aspects as a method of self-defense, the physical conditioning involved with Muay Thai training, the devastating effectiveness as an element of Mixed Martial Arts (MMA) stand-up fighting, and the sport itself. Muay Thai, translated into English as Thai Boxing, is the national sport of Thailand and a martial art with origins in the warfare tactics of the Thai army. It evolved from Krabi Krabong (Krŭ–bē Krŭ–bŏng), the hand-to-hand tactics of the Thai army.

Muay Thai is commonly referred to as the "Art of eight weapons" due to its utilization of eight striking weapons: hands, elbows, shins and knees. Muay Thai also features a unique form of standing grappling called the plum and/or clinch.

The art of Muay Thai is always evolving. There may be differences in teaching styles and variations of techniques, depending on the lineage of instruction. One of the most vivid examples of its evolution is the change from the traditional arm position to its current form resembling Western-style boxing. This positive change affected striking and defensive techniques.

Learning Muay Thai, as with all martial arts, is based on building a strong foundation of basic techniques and then building upon that foundation. As you progress in your training, you can add additional techniques and/or variations that you have learned (e.g., hook kicks, which are not a standard Muay Thai technique, are depicted being used in ancient drawings of Thai fighters).

Muay Thai training methods develop speed, power, and cardio-vascular endurance. Repetition is a very important part of training. Repetition develops "muscle memory," which conditions the body to perform techniques efficiently.

THE BOOK

This book is structured as a learning manual and reference book. It is the perfect companion for new students of Muay Thai who can use the book to learn efficiently, while experienced students can use the book to refine their techniques.

The information is presented in a straightforward way and thoroughly breaks down the mechanics of Muay Thai. Details given include weight distribution, striking area, line of attack, and other important information that allows one to perfect the techniques and be effective. The book includes many learning aids such as photographs, stepping diagrams, tables, training drills, training tips, and more.

The entire book is based on the standard left lead position. Once you have a strong foundation in Muay Thai, you may choose to train from a right lead position. All instruction is given from your perspective facing an opponent unless specifically stated (e.g., opponent's right round kick, inside of opponent's left thigh). Once you understand the body mechanics of a technique, practice it until it is smooth and fluid.

Important points to keep in mind:

- The Muay Thai stance is the heart of the art and all movement and techniques will originate and end with this stance (unless you are engaged in the plum/clinch).

- Stay relaxed during all aspects of Muay Thai. Do not tense up.

- Always keep your chin down and tucked.

- Keep your head moving when in close range. Do not let it be a sitting target.

- When performing a technique, focus on engaging the core muscles of your abdominal area. Consistent training will condition the core muscles and add power to your techniques.

- Focus the full extension of your strikes approximately 2-3 inches behind the target for penetration.

- Do not "pose" after a technique. Always immediately follow-up and/or quickly return to a defensive position.

- POWER = SPEED X MASS

- Nothing is set in stone. All techniques, including footwork, positioning, and defense, can be adjusted to the situation and/or opponent.

DIAGRAMS

CENTERLINE

LEVELS

DIRECTIONAL ANGLES

LINEAR POSITIONING

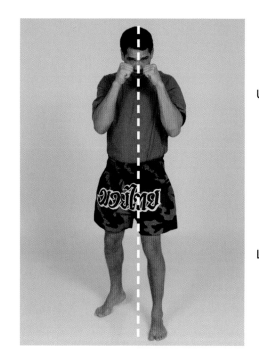

Fig. 1. Centerline
Imaginary axis line down
the center of your body.

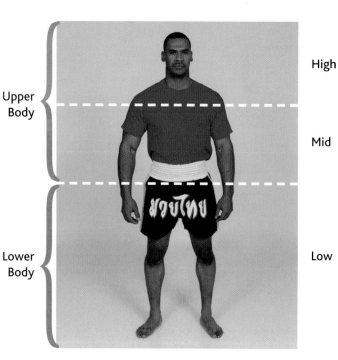

Upper
Body

Lower
Body

High

Mid

Low

Fig. 2. Levels
Height levels pertaining to the body.

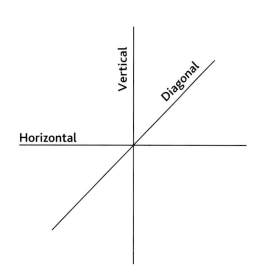

Vertical

Diagonal

Horizontal

Fig. 3. Directional Angles

Fig. 4. Linear Positioning
Positioning the entire left or right side of
the body toward opponent.

MUAY THAI STANCE

Lead Leg

Rear Leg

This is the heart of Muay Thai.

All techniques and movement will originate and end in this stance (unless you are engaged in the plum/clinch).

Keep chin down and tucked at all times, even during techniques and movement.

The Muay Thai stance is a relaxed standing position. Stand up straight, with torso squared off, and relax the shoulders.

Put chin down.

Fists are eye-level and a fist's width apart.

Fists are slightly turned out.

Elbows are down and in toward the torso. (Fig. 5)

Fig. 5.

Fig. 6.

Fists are a fist's width from face. (Fig. 6)

Left leg is in front—**LEAD LEG**
Right leg is behind—**REAR LEG**

Place feet shoulder-width apart.

Point left lead leg and foot straight forward.

Point right rear leg and foot a little to the right at approximately a 45-degree angle with heel up slightly.

Align left lead leg heel and right rear leg toes. (Fig. 7)

Knees will maintain a *very slight* bend.

Weight distribution should be even between both legs.

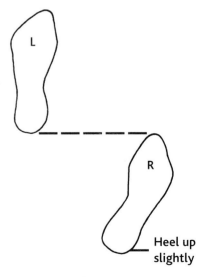

Heel up slightly

Fig. 7.

Fig. 8. Muay Thai stance

The entire book is based on the standard left lead leg position. Once you have a strong foundation in Muay Thai, you may choose to train from a right lead leg position.

MOVEMENT

All movement should be smooth and in a relaxed state.

- With all movement, place feet down toe first, and then heel if needed.

- Always maintain a slight bend in the knees.

FORWARD ADVANCE

From Muay Thai stance, step forward with left lead leg and push forward with right rear leg.

Right rear leg will follow.

End in Muay Thai stance.

Stalking is using the forward advance in a relaxed state to close the distance to opponent and keep constant pressure on opponent.

BACKWARDS RETREAT

From Muay Thai stance, step backwards with right rear leg and push backwards with left lead leg.

Left lead leg will follow.

End in Muay Thai stance.

LATERAL LEFT

From Muay Thai stance, step directly to the left with left lead leg and push to the left with right rear leg.

Right rear leg will follow.

End in Muay Thai stance.

LATERAL RIGHT

From Muay Thai stance, step directly to the right with right rear leg and push to the right with left lead leg.

Left lead leg will follow.

End in Muay Thai stance.

TURN LEFT (QUARTER)

From Muay Thai stance, step one full step forward with right rear leg.

Turn ¼ to the left by pivoting on both the left and right balls of feet.

End in Muay Thai stance.

TURN RIGHT (QUARTER)

From Muay Thai stance, step back and to the left with right rear leg.

Turn ¼ to the right by pivoting on heel of left foot and ball of right foot. (Fig. 9)

End in Muay Thai stance.

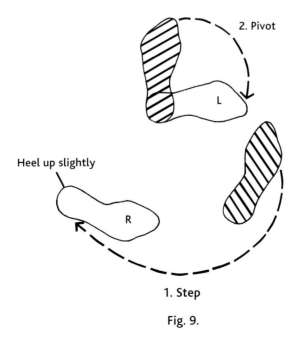

Fig. 9.

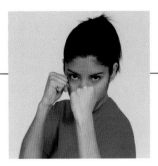

UPPER BODY STRIKES

Jab	Down Elbow (Right)
Cross	Up Elbow (Left)
Hook (Left)	Up Elbow (Right)
Hook (Right)	Spinning Back-Fist (Left)
Low Jab	Spinning Back-Fist (Right)
Low Cross	Spinning Back-Elbow (Left)
Low Hook	Spinning Back-Elbow (Right)
Uppercut (Left)	Jump Fly Cross (Left)
Uppercut (Right)	Jump Fly Cross (Right)
Horizontal Elbow (Left)	Jump Fly Elbow (Left)
Horizontal Elbow (Right)	Jump Fly Elbow (Right)
Down Elbow (Left)	

JAB

The jab is a quick snapping strike.

Advance forward while striking.

From Muay Thai stance, left fist punches eye-level in a straight line directly from hand position.

Roll left shoulder forward into left side of face for coverage of left cheek and chin.

Move right fist against right cheek for coverage of right cheek and chin. (Fig. 10)

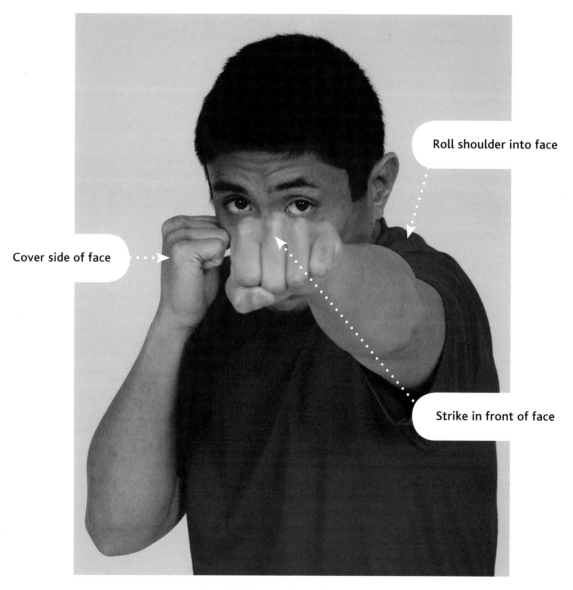

Roll shoulder into face

Cover side of face

Strike in front of face

Fig. 10. Three points of coverage

Roll fist to strike with first two knuckles. At full extension, first two knuckles will align with wrist, arm, and shoulder. (Fig. 11)

Align first two knuckles

Fig. 11. Top View

The strike will move in a direct line to target.

Return to Muay Thai stance.

The jab also can be done from a stationary stance or any direction of movement depending on distance and positioning with target.

CROSS

The cross is a power strike and should be fast and hard.

From Muay Thai stance, punch right fist at eye-level and in a straight line directly from hand position.

Shift 95% of weight onto left lead leg and slightly bend knee of left lead leg.

Pivot right rear leg inward and to the left, thrusting right hip and shoulder toward target by pivoting on ball of right foot. (Fig. 12)

Roll right shoulder forward into right side of face for coverage of right cheek and chin.

Move left fist against left cheek for coverage of left cheek and chin. (Fig. 13)

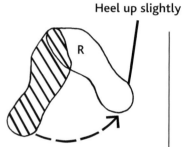

Heel up slightly

Pivot

Fig. 12

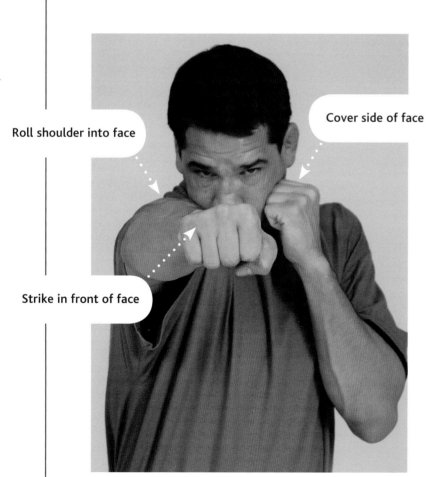

Roll shoulder into face

Cover side of face

Strike in front of face

Fig. 13. Three points of coverage

Roll fist to strike with first two knuckles. At full extension, first two knuckles will align with wrist, arm, and shoulder.

The strike will move in a direct line to target.

Return to Muay Thai stance.

The cross also can be done from any direction of movement depending on distance and positioning with target.

HOOK (LEFT)

The left hook can be used as a fast and snapping strike or power strike.

From Muay Thai stance, raise left elbow eye-level creating a horizontal line with fist.

Fist position is vertical. (Fig. 14)

First two knuckles

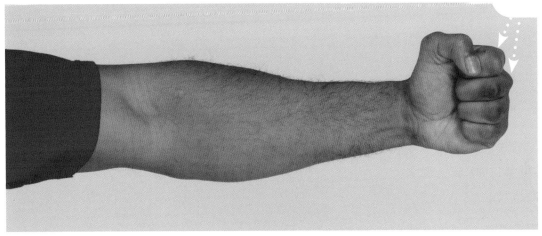

Fig. 14.

Shift 75% of weight to right rear leg. Right heel will go down "flatfooted."

Pivot left lead leg to the right by pivoting on ball of left foot and raising left heel. (Fig. 15)

Heel up slightly

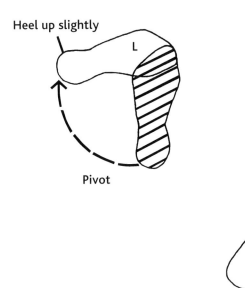

Pivot

Fig. 15.

While pivoting, turn left hip and left side of torso towards opponent to a left linear position. (Fig. 16)

Horizontal fist

Fig. 16.

The strike will move left to right with the force created from pivoting.

Roll left shoulder forward into left side of face for coverage of left cheek and chin.

Move right fist against right cheek for coverage of right cheek and chin.

Strike with first two knuckles which should be aligned with wrist and forearm. (Fig. 14)

Return to Muay Thai stance.

The left hook also can be done from any direction of movement depending on distance and positioning with target.

HOOK (RIGHT)

The right hook can be used as a fast and snapping strike or power strike.

From Muay Thai stance, raise right elbow eye-level to create a horizontal line with fist.

Fist position is vertical. (Fig. 17)

First two knuckles

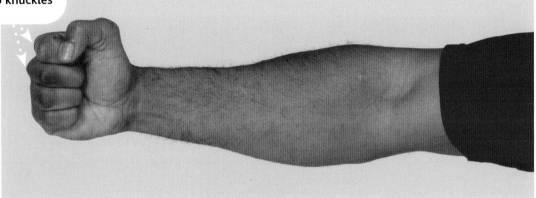

Fig. 17.

Shift 75% of weight to left lead leg.

Pivot right rear leg inward and to the left on ball of right foot. (Fig. 18)

While pivoting, turn right hip and right side of torso toward opponent to a right linear position while maintaining a left lead stance.

The strike will move right to left with the force created by pivoting.

Roll right shoulder forward into right side of face for coverage of right cheek and chin.

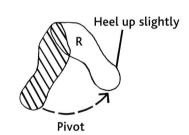

Heel up slightly

Pivot

Fig. 18.

Move left fist against left cheek for coverage of left cheek and chin.

Strike with first two knuckles which should be aligned with wrist and forearm. (Fig. 17)

Return to Muay Thai stance.

The right hook also can be done from any direction of movement depending on distance and positioning with target.

LOW JAB

The low jab is the same as the regular jab technique, but drop eye-level by bending both knees substantially while advancing and striking.

Do not lead with head. Keep back straight and only bend knees to lower level.

Return to Muay Thai stance.

LOW CROSS

The low cross is the same as the regular cross technique, but drop eye-level by bending both knees substantially while striking.

Do not lead with head. Keep back straight and only bend knees to lower level.

Return to Muay Thai stance.

LOW HOOK (LEFT AND RIGHT)

The low hook is the same as the regular hook (left and right) technique, but drop eye-level by bending both knees substantially while striking.

Do not lead with head. Keep back straight and only bend knees to lower level.

Return to Muay Thai stance.

UPPERCUT (LEFT)

The left uppercut is a fast snapping strike.

From Muay Thai stance, shift 95% of weight to left lead leg.

Bend both knees approximately 6 inches.

Roll right shoulder forward and dip left shoulder slightly.

Strike with left fist on the centerline, low to high. (Fig. 19)

While striking, rotate left fist so palm is facing you. (Fig. 20)

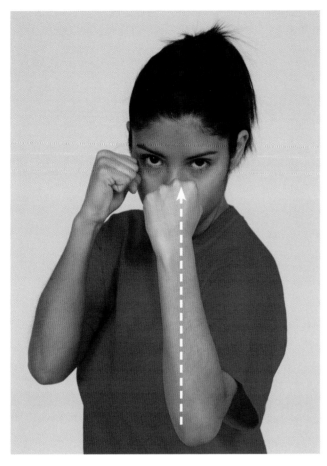

Push up with left lead leg and thrust left shoulder up and forward during the strike.

Keep left outer forearm close to opponent and on centerline during the strike.

Move right fist against right cheek for coverage of right cheek and chin.

Strike with first two knuckles which should be aligned with wrist and forearm. (Fig. 21)

Return to Muay Thai stance.

The left uppercut also can be done from any direction of movement depending on distance and positioning with target.

Fig. 19.

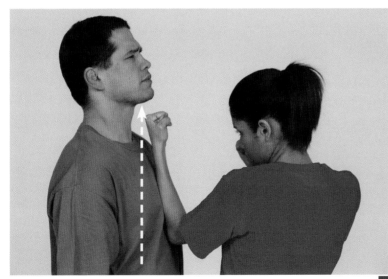

Fig. 20.

First two knuckles

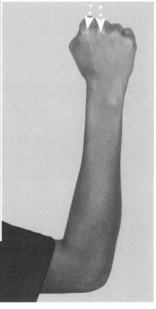

Fig. 21.

UPPERCUT (RIGHT)

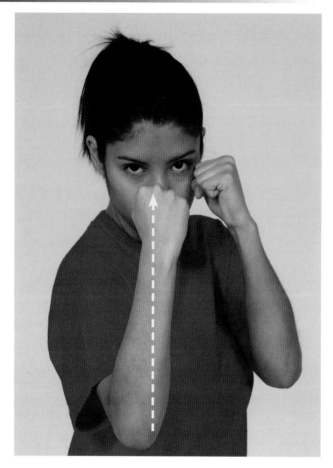

Fig. 22.

The right uppercut is a fast snapping strike.

From Muay Thai stance, shift 95% of weight to right rear leg.

Bend both knees approximately 6 inches.

Roll left shoulder forward and dip right shoulder slightly.

Strike with right fist on the centerline, low to high. (Fig. 22)

While striking, rotate right fist so palm is facing you.

Push up with right rear leg and thrust right shoulder up and forward during the strike.

Keep right outer forearm close to opponent and on centerline during the strike.

Move left fist against left cheek for coverage of left cheek and chin.

Strike with first two knuckles which should be aligned with wrist and forearm. (Fig. 23)

Return to Muay Thai stance.

The right uppercut also can be done from any direction of movement depending on distance and positioning with target.

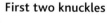

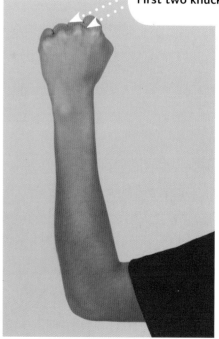

First two knuckles

Fig. 23. First two knuckles

HORIZONTAL ELBOW (LEFT)

The left horizontal elbow is a fast snapping strike.

From Muay Thai stance, raise both elbows so fists are forehead-level.

Move right arm slightly to the left and rotate forearm out (palm away) for coverage.

Lift left elbow up to align horizontal with left fist and rotate forearm out (palm away). (Fig. 24)

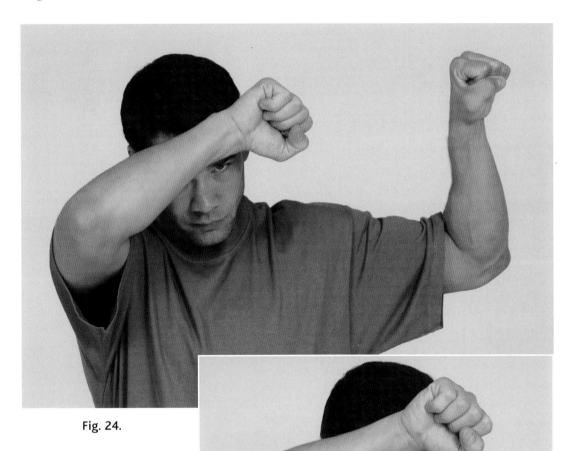

Fig. 24.

Strike by snapping point of left elbow forward to centerline. **Do not over extend past centerline.**

Relax left hand so it can bend at wrist against center of chest. (Fig. 25)

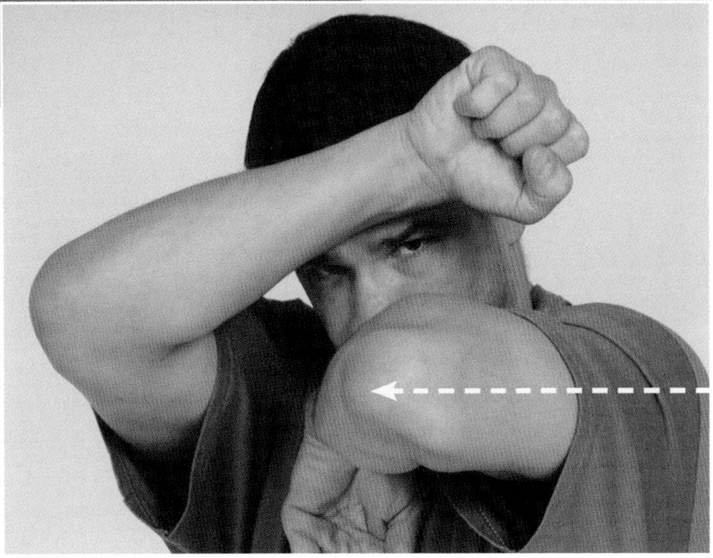

Fig. 25.

Thrust left shoulder forward slightly and shift 75% of weight to right rear leg while striking.

Pivot left lead leg inward and to the right on ball of left foot and raise left heel during the strike. (Fig. 26)

The strike will move left to right in a horizontal line.

The strike can be used to rip and tear with the point of the elbow or hit with the bottom three inches of the outer forearm near the elbow. (Fig. 27)

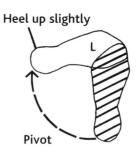

Heel up slightly

L

Pivot

R

Fig. 26.

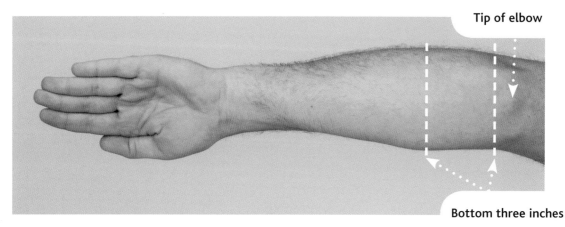

Tip of elbow

Bottom three inches

Fig. 27.

Return to Muay Thai stance.

The left horizontal elbow also can be done from any direction of movement depending on distance and positioning with target.

HORIZONTAL ELBOW (RIGHT)

The right horizontal elbow is a fast snapping strike.

From Muay Thai stance, raise both elbows so fists are forehead-level.

Move left arm slightly to the right and rotate forearm out (palm away) for coverage.

Lift right elbow up to align horizontal with right fist and rotate forearm out (palm away). (Fig. 28)

Fig. 28.

Strike by snapping point of right elbow forward to centerline. **Do not over extend past centerline.**

Relax right hand so it can bend at wrist against center of chest. (Fig. 29)

Thrust right shoulder forward slightly and shift 75% of weight to left lead leg while striking.

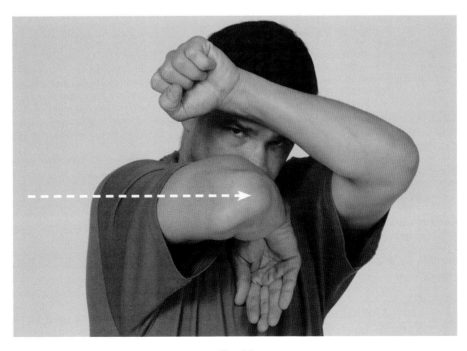

Fig. 29.

Pivot right rear leg inward and to the left on ball of right foot and raise right heel during the strike. (Fig. 30)

The strike will move right to left in a horizontal line.

The strike can be used to rip and tear with the point of the elbow or hit with the bottom three inches of the outer forearm near the elbow. (Fig. 31)

Return to Muay Thai stance.

The right horizontal elbow also can be done from any direction of movement depending on distance and positioning with target.

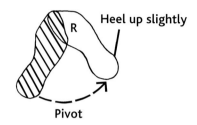

Fig. 30.

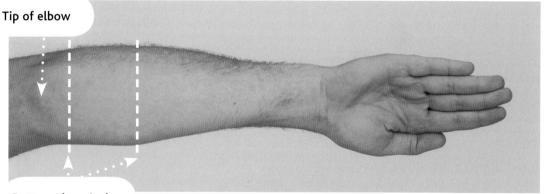

Tip of elbow

Bottom three inches

Fig. 31.

DOWN ELBOW (LEFT)

The left down elbow is a fast snapping strike.

From Muay Thai stance, raise both elbows so fists are forehead-level.

Move right arm slightly to the left and rotate forearm out (palm away) for coverage.

Lift left elbow straight up dropping left fist to align elbow and fist as vertical as possible and rotate forearm out (palm away). (Fig.32)

Strike by snapping point of left elbow downward on centerline.

Relax left hand so it can bend at wrist against center of chest. (Fig.33)

Fig. 32.

Thrust left shoulder forward slightly and shift 75% of weight to right rear leg while striking.

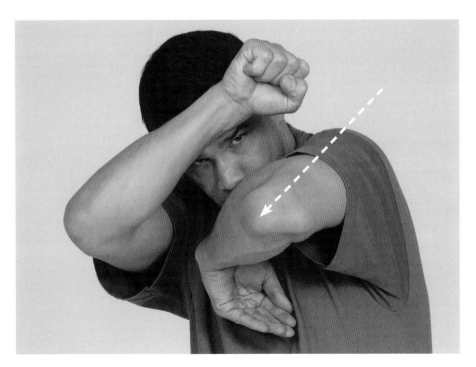

Fig. 33.

Pivot left lead leg inward and to the right on ball of left foot and raise left heel during the strike. (Fig. 34)

The strike will move high to low on centerline.

The strike can be used to rip and tear with the point of the elbow or hit with the bottom three inches of the outer forearm near the elbow. (Fig. 35)

Return to Muay Thai stance.

The left down elbow also can be done from any direction of movement depending on distance and positioning with target.

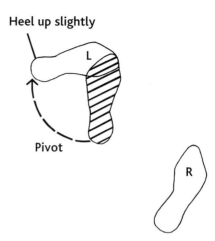

Heel up slightly

Pivot

Fig. 34.

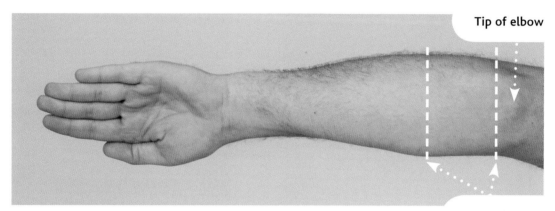

Tip of elbow

Bottom three inches

Fig. 35.

DOWN ELBOW (RIGHT)

The right down elbow is a fast snapping strike.

From Muay Thai stance, raise both elbows so fists are forehead-level.

Move left arm slightly to the right and rotate forearm out (palm away) for coverage.

Lift right elbow straight up dropping right fist to align elbow and fist as vertical as possible and rotate forearm out (palm away). (Fig. 36)

Strike by snapping point of right elbow downward on centerline.

Fig. 36.

Relax right hand so it can bend at wrist against center of chest. (Fig. 37)

Thrust right shoulder forward slightly and shift 75% of weight to left lead leg while striking.

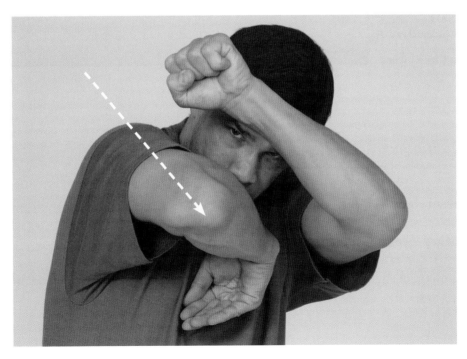

Fig. 37.

Pivot right rear leg inward and to the left on ball of right foot and raise right heel during the strike. (Fig. 38)

The strike will move high to low on center-line.

The strike can be used to rip and tear with the point of the elbow or hit with the bottom three inches of the outer forearm near the elbow. (Fig. 39)

Return to Muay Thai stance.

The right down elbow also can be done from any direction of movement depending on distance and positioning with target.

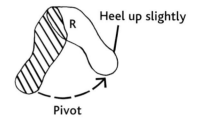

Heel up slightly

Pivot

Fig. 38.

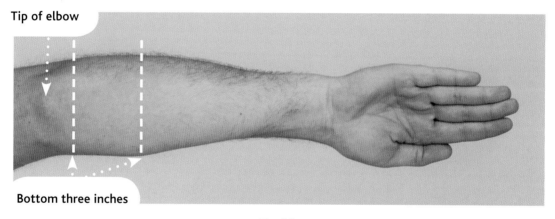

Tip of elbow

Bottom three inches

Fig. 39

UP ELBOW (LEFT)

The left up elbow is a fast snapping strike.

From Muay Thai stance, raise right elbow so right fist is forehead-level.

Move right arm slightly to the left and rotate forearm out (palm away) for coverage.

Left elbow will strike from original position.

Strike by snapping point of left elbow upward on centerline.

Fig. 40.

Relax left hand so it can bend at wrist against center of chest.

Thrust left shoulder forward substantially to raise elbow to eye-level and twist upper body to an almost left linear position. (Fig. 40)

Shift 75% of weight to right rear leg while striking.

Pivot left lead leg inward and to the right on ball of left foot and raise left heel during the strike. (Fig. 41)

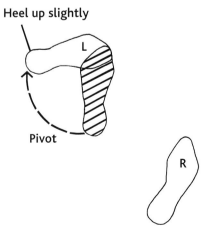

Fig. 41.

The strike will move low to high on centerline.

The strike can be used to rip and tear with the point of the elbow or hit with the bottom three inches of the outer forearm near the elbow. (Fig. 42)

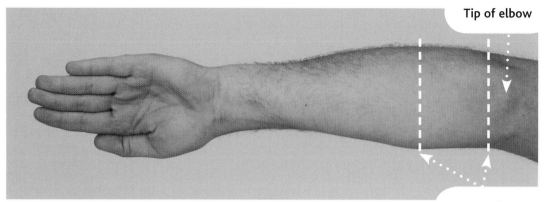

Tip of elbow

Bottom three inches

Fig. 42.

Return to Muay Thai stance.

The left up elbow also can be done from any direction of movement depending on distance and positioning with target.

UP ELBOW (RIGHT)

The right up elbow is a fast snapping strike.

From Muay Thai stance, raise left elbow so left fist is forehead-level.

Move left arm slightly to the right and rotate forearm out (palm away) for coverage.

Right elbow will strike from original position.

Strike by snapping point of right elbow upward on centerline.

Relax right hand so it can bend at wrist against center of chest.

Thrust right shoulder forward substantially to raise elbow to eye-level and twist upper body to an almost right linear position. (Fig. 43)

Shift 75% of weight to left lead leg while striking.

Pivot right rear leg inward and to the left on ball of right foot and raise right heel during the strike. (Fig. 44)

Fig. 43.

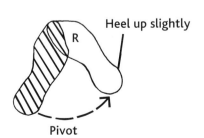

Fig. 44.

The strike will move low to high on centerline.

The strike can be used to rip and tear with the point of the elbow or hit with the bottom three inches of the outer forearm near the elbow. (Fig. 45)

Tip of elbow

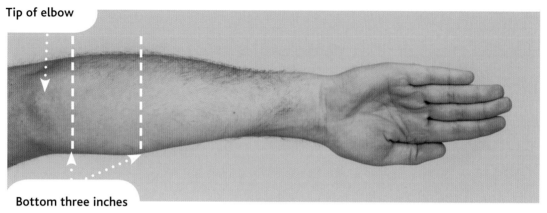

Bottom three inches

Fig. 45.

Return to Muay Thai stance.

The right up elbow also can be done from any direction of movement depending on distance and positioning with target.

SPINNING BACK-FIST (LEFT)

The left spinning back-fist is a fast power strike using centrifugal force.

From Muay Thai stance, take a full step forward and to the left across the body and past centerline with right rear leg.

Drop 100% of weight to right leg.

Lift left foot slightly off ground and spin counter-clockwise by pivoting on ball of right foot.

Left leg will land in original left lead leg position facing opponent. (Fig. 46)

Turn head to the left to keep visual contact with opponent during the spin.

Strike with left fist while spinning.

Straighten left arm during spin. **Leave a slight bend in elbow.**

Slightly bend left wrist to position first two knuckles ahead of arm. (Fig. 47)

Power is created by the speed and centrifugal force of the spin.

Move right fist against right cheek for coverage of right cheek and chin.

The strike will move right to left in a horizontal line.

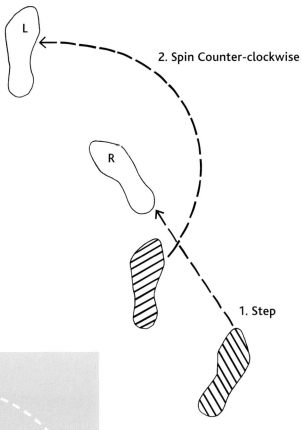

2. Spin Counter-clockwise

1. Step

Fig. 46.

Strike with first two knuckles from backside of fist.

Return to Muay Thai stance facing opponent.

Knuckles ahead of arm

Slight bend in elbow

Fig. 47. Top View

SPINNING BACK-FIST (RIGHT)

The right spinning back-fist is a fast power strike using centrifugal force.

From Muay Thai stance, take a full step forward and to the right across the body and past centerline with left lead leg.

Drop 100% of weight to left leg.

Lift right foot slightly off ground and spin clockwise by pivoting on ball of left foot.

Right leg will spin completely around and land in original right rear leg position. (Fig. 48)

Turn head to the right to keep visual contact with opponent during the spin.

Strike with right fist while spinning.

Straighten right arm during spin. **Leave a slight bend in elbow.**

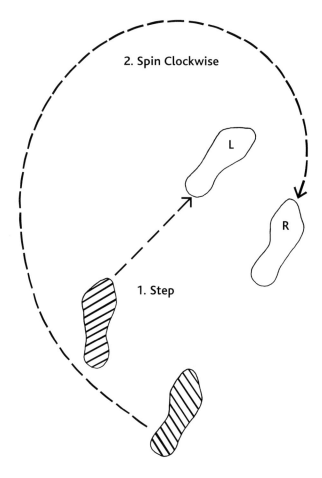

Fig. 48.

Slightly bend right wrist to position first two knuckles ahead of arm. (Fig. 49)

Power is created by the speed and centrifugal force of the spin.

Move left fist against left cheek for coverage of left cheek and chin.

The strike will move left to right in a horizontal line.

Strike with first two knuckles from backside of fist.

Return to Muay Thai stance facing opponent.

Knuckles ahead of arm

Slight bend in elbow

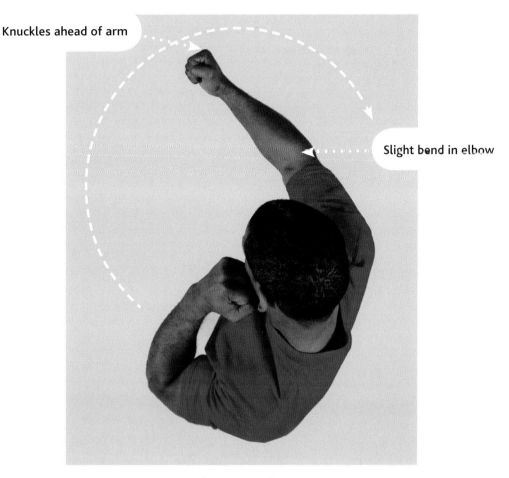

Fig. 49. Top view

SPINNING BACK-ELBOW (LEFT)

The left spinning back-elbow is a fast power strike using centrifugal force.

From Muay Thai stance, take a full step forward and to the left across the body and past centerline with right rear leg.

Drop 100% of weight to right leg.

Lift left foot slightly off ground and spin counter-clockwise by pivoting on ball of right foot.

Left leg will land in original left lead leg position facing opponent. (Fig. 50)

Turn head to the left to keep visual contact with opponent during the spin.

Raise both elbows so fists are forehead-level.

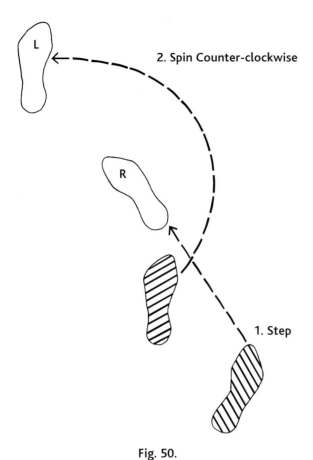

2. Spin Counter-clockwise

1. Step

Fig. 50.

Move right arm slightly to the left and rotate forearm out (palm away) for coverage.

Lift left elbow straight up dropping left fist to align elbow and fist as vertically as possible and rotate forearm out (palm away). (Fig. 51)

Power is created by the speed and centrifugal force of the spin.

The strike will move right to left and high to low in a diagonal line.

Strike with bottom three inches of back of elbow or point of elbow for ripping and tearing. (Fig. 52)

Options after impact for distance: 1) continue counter-clockwise pivoting to Muay Thai stance facing opponent, or 2) reverse pivot clockwise and step back with right leg to return to Muay Thai stance facing opponent.

Fig. 51.

Fig. 52.

SPINNING BACK-ELBOW (RIGHT)

The right spinning back-elbow is a fast power strike using centrifugal force.

From Muay Thai stance, take a full step forward and to the right across the body and past centerline with left lead leg.

Drop 100% of weight to left leg.

Lift right foot slightly off ground and spin clockwise by pivoting on ball of left foot.

Right leg will spin completely around and land in original right rear leg position. (Fig. 53)

Turn head to the right to keep visual contact with opponent during the spin.

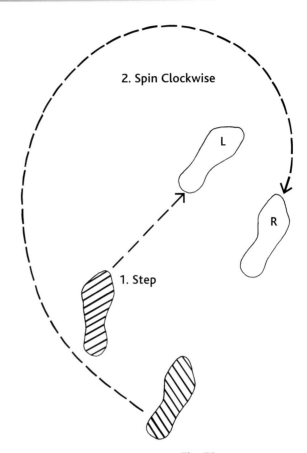

Fig. 53.

Fig. 54.

Raise both elbows so fists are forehead-level.

Move left arm slightly to the right and rotate forearm out (palm away) for coverage.

Lift right elbow straight up dropping right fist to align elbow and fist as vertically as possible and rotate forearm out (palm away). (Fig. 54)

Power is created by the speed and centrifugal force of the spin.

The strike will move left to right and high to low in a diagonal line.

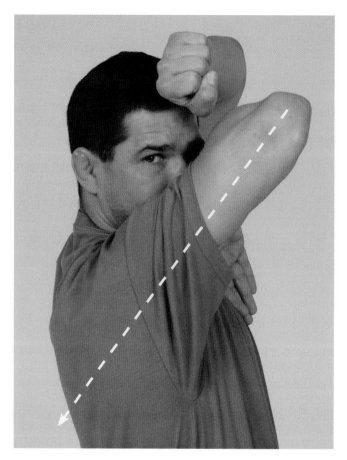

Fig. 55.

Strike with bottom three inches of back of elbow or point of elbow for ripping and tearing. (Fig. 55)

Options after impact for distance: 1) continue clockwise pivoting to Muay Thai stance facing opponent, or 2) reverse pivot counter-clockwise to return to Muay Thai stance facing opponent.

JUMP FLY CROSS (LEFT)

The left jump fly cross is a power strike used to close the distance between you and the target while striking with added momentum.

From Muay Thai stance, **switch step**—Quickly switch both feet without moving forward, drop 100% of weight on to right leg and bend right knee. (Fig. 56)

Jump forward and up by pushing off right leg.

The jump will have an arch ending at the impact point with target. (Fig. 57)

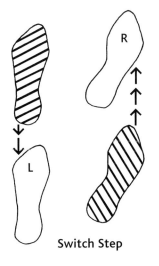

Switch Step

Fig. 56.

Strike with the left cross using the downward momentum from the end of the jump.

Left fist punches at eye-level and in a straight line directly from hand position.

Roll left shoulder forward into left side of face for coverage of left cheek and chin.

Move right fist against right cheek for coverage of right cheek and chin.

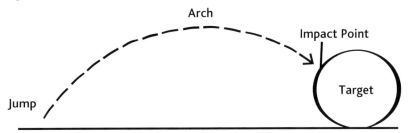

Fig. 57.

Kick left leg backwards during the strike to increase momentum.

Roll fist to strike with first two knuckles. At full extension, first two knuckles will align with wrist, arm, and shoulder. (Fig. 58)

The strike will move in a direct line to target.

Land on right leg.

Return to Muay Thai stance facing opponent.

Kick leg back

Fig. 58.

JUMP FLY CROSS (RIGHT)

The right jump fly cross is a power strike used to close the distance between you and the target while striking with added momentum.

From Muay Thai stance, **stutter step**—Lean forward placing 100% of weight on left lead leg.

Maintaining full balance with left lead leg, move right rear leg one full step forward slightly off the ground but do not touch right foot down, then quickly switch both feet **without moving forward.**

Keep 100% of weight on left lead leg and bend left knee. (Fig. 59)

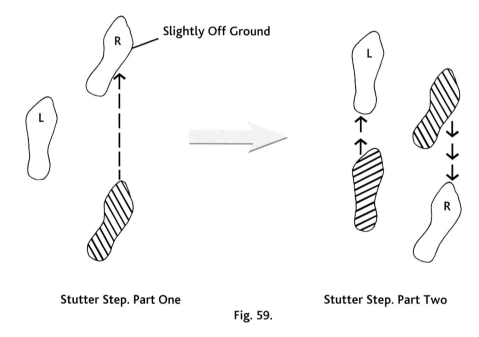

Stutter Step. Part One   Stutter Step. Part Two

Fig. 59.

Jump forward and up by pushing off left lead leg.

The jump will have an arch ending at the impact point with target. (Fig. 60)

Strike with the right cross using the down momentum from the end of the jump.

Right fist punches at eye-level and in a straight line directly from hand position.

Roll right shoulder forward into right side of face for coverage of right cheek and chin.

Move left fist against left cheek for coverage of left cheek and chin.

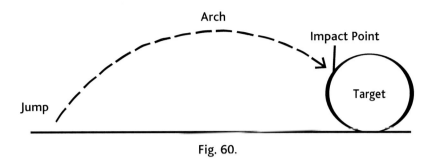

Fig. 60.

Kick right leg backwards during the strike to increase momentum.

Roll fist to strike with first two knuckles. At full extension, first two knuckles will align with wrist, arm, and shoulder. (Fig. 61)

The strike will move in a direct line to target.

Land on left leg.

Return to Muay Thai stance facing opponent.

Fig. 61.

JUMP FLY ELBOW (LEFT)

The left jump fly elbow is a power strike used to close the distance between you and the target while striking with added momentum.

From Muay Thai stance, **switch step**—Quickly switch both feet without moving forward, drop 100% of weight on to right leg and bend right knee. (Fig. 62)

Jump forward and up by pushing off right leg.

The jump will have an arch ending at the impact point with target. (Fig. 63)

Strike with left down elbow using the down momentum from the end of the jump.

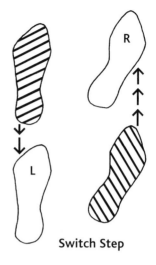

Switch Step

Fig. 62.

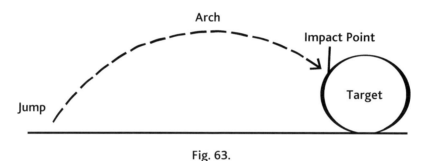

Fig. 63.

Raise both elbows so fists are forehead-level.

Move right arm slightly to the left and rotate forearm out (palm away) for coverage.

Lift left elbow straight up dropping left fist to align elbow and fist as vertically as possible and rotate forearm out (palm away).

Strike by snapping point of left elbow downward on centerline.

Relax left hand so it can bend at wrist against center of chest.

Thrust left shoulder forward slightly during the strike.

Kick left leg backwards during the strike to increase momentum. (Fig. 64)

Kick leg back

Fig. 64.

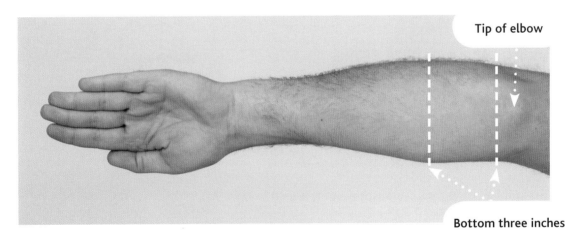

Tip of elbow

Bottom three inches

Fig. 65.

The strike will move high to low on centerline.

The strike can be used to rip and tear with the point of the elbow or hit with the bottom three inches of the outer forearm near the elbow. (Fig. 65)

Land on right leg.

Return to Muay Thai stance facing opponent.

JUMP FLY ELBOW (RIGHT)

The right jump fly elbow is a power strike used to close the distance between you and the target while striking with added momentum.

From Muay Thai stance, **stutter step**—Lean forward placing 100% of weight on left lead leg.

Maintaining full balance with left lead leg, move right rear leg one full step forward slightly off the ground but do not touch right foot down, then quickly switch both feet without moving forward.

Keep 100% of weight on left lead leg and bend left knee. (Fig. 66)

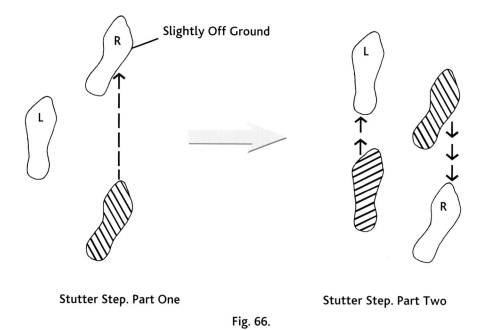

Stutter Step. Part One   Stutter Step. Part Two

Fig. 66.

Jump forward and up by pushing off left lead leg.

The jump will have an arch ending at the impact point with target. (Fig. 67)

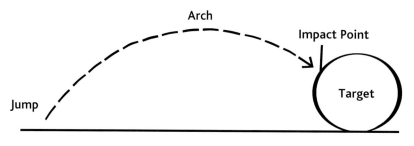

Fig. 67.

Strike with right down elbow using the down momentum from the end of the jump.

Raise both elbows so fists are forehead-level.

Move left arm slightly to the right and rotate forearm out (palm away) for coverage.

Lift right elbow straight up dropping right fist to align elbow and fist as vertically as possible and rotate forearm out (palm away).

Strike by snapping point of right elbow downward on centerline.

Relax right hand so it can bend at wrist against center of chest.

Kick leg back

Fig. 68.

Thrust right shoulder forward slightly during the strike.

Kick right leg backwards during the strike to increase momentum. (Fig. 68)

The strike will move high to low on centerline.

The strike can be used to rip and tear with the point of the elbow or hit with the bottom three inches of the outer forearm near the elbow. (Fig. 69)

Land on left leg.

Return to Muay Thai stance facing opponent.

Tip of elbow

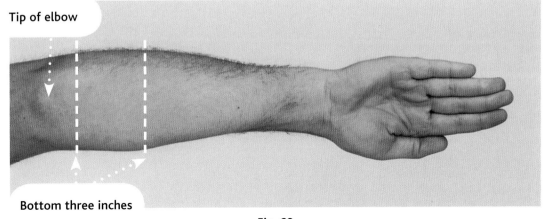

Bottom three inches

Fig. 69.

LOWER BODY STRIKES

Left Round Kick

Right Round Kick

Cut Kick (Left)

Cut Kick (Right)

Left Angle Kick

Right Angle Kick

Long Foot Jab

Short Foot Jab

Long Knee (Left)

Long Knee (Right)

Jump Fly Knee (Left)

Jump Fly Knee (Right)

LEFT ROUND KICK

The left round kick is a fast power strike.

From Muay Thai stance, step right rear leg one full step forward and to the right in a diagonal line. Drop 100% of weight on right lead leg. (Fig. 70)

Using the forward momentum from the step, push off left foot and swing left leg forward at desired height. Bend left knee slightly and align shin horizontally and flush with target.

Pivot to the right on ball of right foot.

Rotate right arm palm out and move to the left across centerline and above eye line. Touch outer forearm across forehead for coverage.

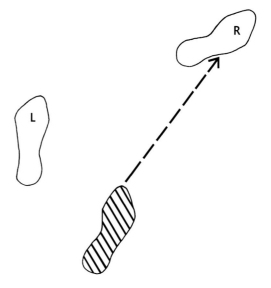

Fig. 70.

You may drop the right fist and forearm from this position to cover the left cheek and chin, if needed.

Throw left arm behind left leg during the strike for added momentum. (Fig. 71)

Strike with left shin.

The strike can be used at any height, low to high.

The strike will move from left to right.

After the impact, place left leg behind you and step back with right leg to return to Muay Thai stance.

If no impact, stop momentum by "scooping" the kick—bend and lift left knee and place left leg behind you. Step back with right leg to Muay Thai stance.

The left round kick also can be done from a stationary stance, switch step, or right lateral movement depending on distance and positioning with target.

Fig. 71.

RIGHT ROUND KICK

The right round kick is a fast power strike.

From Muay Thai stance, left lead leg steps forward and to the left in a diagonal line. Drop 100% of weight on left lead leg. (Fig. 72)

Using the forward momentum from the step, push off right foot and swing right leg forward at desired height. Bend right knee slightly and align shin horizontally and flush with target.

Pivot to the left on ball of left foot.

Rotate left arm palm out and move to the right across centerline and above eye line. Touch outer forearm across forehead for coverage.

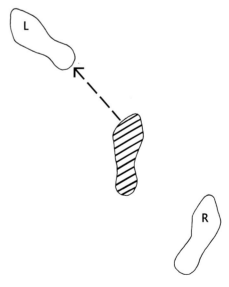

Fig. 72.

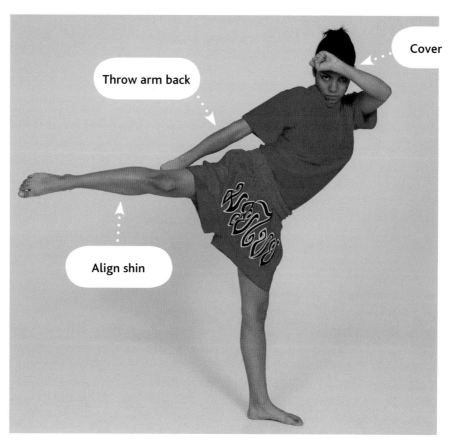

Fig. 73.

You may drop the left fist and forearm from this position to cover the right cheek and chin, if needed.

Throw right arm behind right leg during the strike for added momentum. (Fig. 73)

Strike with right shin.

The strike can be used at any height, low to high.

The strike will move from right to left.

After the impact, place right leg behind you to return to Muay Thai stance.

If no impact, arch the right kick to a downward angle and continue spinning counter-clockwise to return to Muay Thai stance. Keep eyes on opponent by turning head during the spin.

The right round kick also can be done from a stationary stance, stutter step, or left lateral movement depending on distance and positioning with target.

CUT KICK (LEFT)

The left cut kick is the same technique as the left round kick, but drop eye-level by bending right knee substantially while stepping and striking.

Do not lead with head. Keep back straight and only bend right knee to lower level.

After the impact, place left leg behind you and step back with right leg to return to Muay Thai stance.

Options for target are: 1) inside of opponent's left leg at the knee or inner thigh, or 2) outside of opponent's right leg at the knee or outer thigh, depending on distance and positioning.

Options for the striking angle are: 1) up, 2) down, or 3) horizontal.

Return to Muay Thai stance.

The left cut kick can be used as a strike or to disrupt opponent's right round kick by throwing opponent off balance (Kick opponent's left base leg).

CUT KICK (RIGHT)

The right cut kick is the same technique as the right round kick, but drop eye-level by bending left knee substantially while stepping and striking.

Do not lead with head. Keep back straight and only bend left knee to lower level.

After the impact, place right leg behind you to Muay Thai stance.

Options for target are: 1) inside of opponent's right leg at the knee or inner thigh, or 2) outside of opponent's left leg at the knee or outer thigh, depending on distance and positioning.

Options for the striking angle are: 1) up, 2) down, or 3) horizontal.

Return to Muay Thai stance.

The right cut kick can be used as a strike or to disrupt opponent's left round kick by throwing opponent off balance (Kick opponent's right base leg).

LEFT ANGLE KICK

The left angle kick is a quick, snapping strike.

Remain stationary throughout technique.

From Muay Thai stance, drop 100% of weight on right rear leg. Left lead leg will quickly shoot in a slight diagonal line up and to the right. Bend knee slightly and align shin with target. Pivot to the right on ball of right foot.

Rotate right arm palm out and move to the left across centerline and above eye line. Touch outer forearm across forehead for coverage.

You may drop the right fist and forearm from this position to cover the left cheek and chin, if needed.

Snap left arm behind left leg during the strike for added momentum. (Fig. 74)

Strike with left shin.

The strike can be used at any height, low to high.

The strike will move from left to right in an upward diagonal line.

After the strike, quickly place left leg down to return to Muay Thai stance.

Using the angle of the left angle kick, you can go under opponent's right arm to target opponent's ribs.

Fig. 74.

RIGHT ANGLE KICK

The right angle kick is a quick, snapping strike.

Remain stationary throughout technique.

From Muay Thai stance, drop 100% of weight on left lead leg. Quickly shoot right rear leg in a slight diagonal line up and to the left. Bend knee slightly and align shin with target. Pivot to the left on ball of left foot.

Rotate left arm palm out and move to the right across centerline and above eye line. Touch outer forearm across forehead for coverage.

You may drop the left fist and forearm from this position to cover the right cheek and chin, if needed.

Snap right arm behind right leg during the strike for added momentum. (Fig. 75)

Strike with right shin.

The strike can be used at any height, low to high.

The strike will move from right to left in an upward diagonal line.

After the strike, quickly place right leg behind you to return to Muay Thai stance.

Using the angle of the right angle kick, you can go under opponent's left arm to target opponent's ribs.

Fig. 75.

LONG FOOT JAB

The long foot jab is a pushing technique or a quick thrusting strike.

From Muay Thai stance, shift 100% of weight to right leg and lift left leg up by raising and bending knee. (Fig. 76)

Pushing technique: Thrust left leg forward, make contact with entire bottom of foot in a direct line and push target. (Fig. 77)

Striking technique: Thrust left leg forward quickly, point left foot forward and pull toes back to strike with ball of left foot. Strike in a direct line. At full extension, ball of left foot will be in a direct line with left knee and hip. (Fig. 78)

Push forward with right foot and slide right foot forward for distance and added momentum.

Fig. 76.

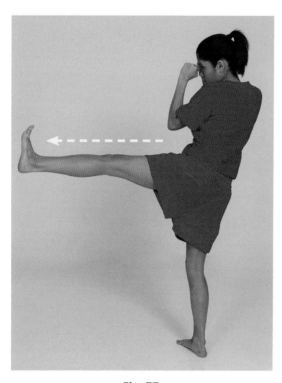

Fig. 77.

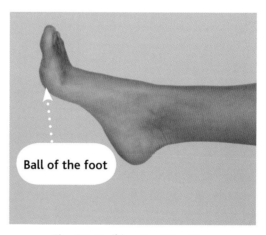

Ball of the foot

Fig. 78. Striking Foot Position

Stay squared off to opponent during the technique and stand up straight. Do not lean upper torso. Do not pivot.

Do not drop hands. Both arms will remain in original position during the entire technique.

Maintain balance with right leg throughout technique.

The strike will move in a direct line to target.

Do not let left leg drop or fall after the impact. Re-bend and lift knee, then place left leg down in Muay Thai stance.

The long foot jab also can be done from a stationary position without sliding the right foot forward.

The long foot jab can be used to push to create distance, stop opponent's forward momentum, disrupt opponent's technique by pushing off balance, or strike, if in range.

Target on opponent can be the chest, stomach, waist, hips, upper legs, or head.

SHORT FOOT JAB

The short foot jab is a pushing technique or a quick thrusting strike.

From Muay Thai stance, shift 100% of weight to left leg. Lift right leg up by raising and bending knee.

Pushing technique: Thrust right leg forward, make contact with entire bottom of foot in a direct line and push target. Thrust right hip forward slightly during the technique. (Fig. 79)

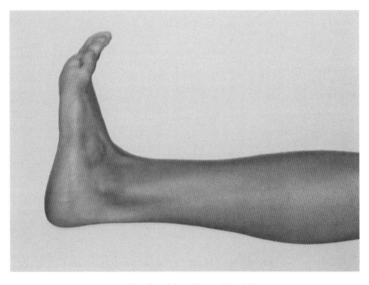

Fig. 79. Pushing Foot Position

Fig. 80. Striking foot position

Striking technique: Thrust right leg forward quickly, point right foot forward and pull toes back to strike with ball of right foot. Strike in a direct line. At full extension, ball of right foot will be in a direct line with right knee and hip. Thrust right hip forward slightly during the strike. (Fig. 80)

Pivot left foot to the left on ball of left foot.

Stay squared off to opponent during the technique and stand up straight. Do not lean upper torso. Do not pivot.

Do not drop hands. Both arms will remain in original position during the entire technique.

Maintain balance with left leg throughout technique.

The strike will move in a direct line to target.

Do not let right leg drop or fall after the impact. Re-bend and lift knee, then place right leg behind you in Muay Thai stance.

You have the option of not pivoting and staying stationary, or not pivoting and using the forward momentum during the technique to slide the left foot forward for distance and added momentum.

The short foot jab can be used to push to create distance, stop opponent's forward momentum, disrupt opponent's technique by pushing off balance, or strike, if in range.

Target on opponent can be the chest, stomach, waist, hips, upper legs, or head.

LONG KNEE (LEFT)

The left long knee is a power strike.

From Muay Thai stance, step one full step straight forward with right rear leg.

Drop 100% of weight to right leg.

Pivot to the right on ball of right foot.

Right foot will raise right heel during the strike and be completely on ball of right foot.

Lift and bend left knee while thrusting it forward directly at target.

Left foot will point toes down. (Fig. 81)

While pivoting, turn left hip and left side of torso toward opponent to a left linear position.

Maintain balance with right leg throughout technique.

Throw left arm behind left leg during the strike for added momentum.

Roll left shoulder into left side of face for coverage of left cheek and chin.

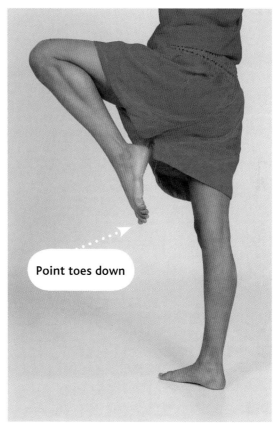

Point toes down

Fig. 81.

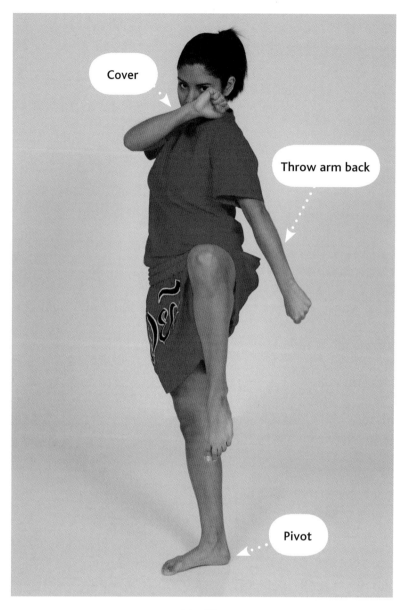

Fig. 82.

Move right arm to the left across centerline against left cheek for further coverage of left cheek and chin. (Fig. 82)

The strike will move in a direct line to target.

Strike with kneecap.

After the strike, place left leg behind you and step back with right leg in Muay Thai stance.

The left long knee also can be done from a switch step.

LONG KNEE (RIGHT)

The right long knee is a power strike.

From Muay Thai stance, shift 100% of weight to left leg.

Pivot to the left on ball of left foot.

Left foot will raise left heel during the strike and be completely on ball of left foot.

Lift and bend right knee while thrusting it forward directly at target.

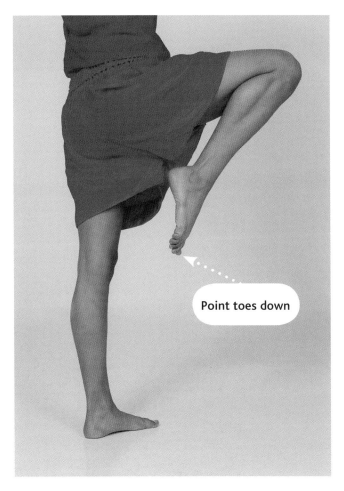

Point toes down

Fig. 83.

Right foot will point toes down. (Fig. 83)

While pivoting, turn right hip and right side of torso toward opponent to a right linear position.

Maintain balance with left leg throughout technique.

Throw right arm behind right leg during the strike for added momentum.

Roll right shoulder into right side of face for coverage of right cheek and chin.

Move left arm to the right across centerline against right cheek for further coverage of right cheek and chin. (Fig. 84)

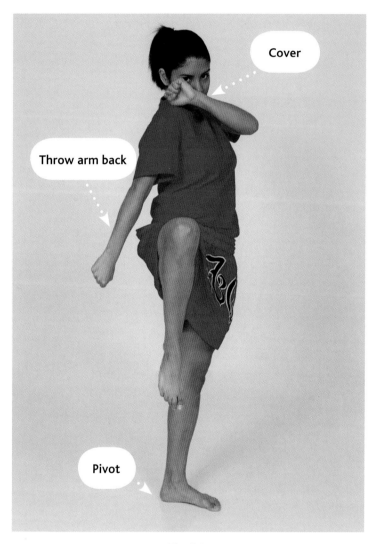

Fig. 84.

The strike will move in a direct line to target.

Strike with kneecap.

After the strike, place right leg behind you in Muay Thai stance.

The right long knee also can be done from a stutter step.

JUMP FLY KNEE (LEFT)

The left jump fly knee is a power strike and used to close the distance between you and the target while striking with added momentum.

From Muay Thai stance, **switch step**—Quickly switch both feet without moving forward, drop 100% of weight on to right leg and bend right knee. (Fig. 85)

Jump forward and up by pushing off right leg.

The impact point will be at the peak of the jump. (Fig. 86)

The left jump fly knee is essentially a left long knee.

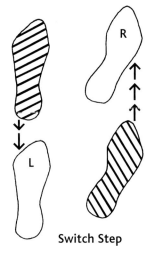

Switch Step

Fig. 85.

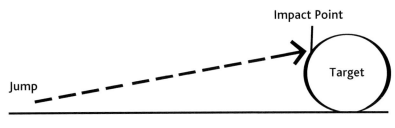

Fig. 86.

Bend left knee while thrusting it forward directly at target.

Left foot will point toes down.

Turn left hip and left side of torso toward opponent to a left linear position.

Throw left arm behind left leg during the strike for added momentum.

Roll left shoulder into left side of face for coverage of left cheek and chin.

Move right arm to the left across centerline against left cheek for further coverage of left cheek and chin. (Fig. 87)

The strike will move in a direct line to target.

Strike with kneecap.

Land on right leg.

Return to Muay Thai stance facing opponent.

Fig. 87.

JUMP FLY KNEE (RIGHT)

The right jump fly knee is a power strike and used to close the distance between you and the target while striking with added momentum.

From Muay Thai stance, **stutter step**—Lean forward placing 100% of weight on left lead leg.

Maintaining full balance with left lead leg, move right rear leg one full step forward slightly off the ground, but do not touch the right foot down, then quickly switch both feet without moving forward. Keep 100% of weight on left lead leg and bend left knee. (Fig. 88)

Jump forward and up by pushing off left leg.

The impact point will be at the peak of the jump. (Fig. 89)

The right jump fly knee is essentially a right long knee.

Bend right knee while thrusting it forward directly at target.

Right foot will point toes down.

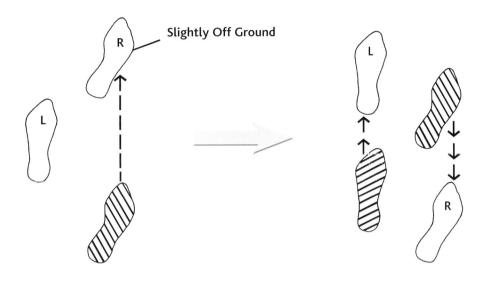

Stutter Step. Part One

Stutter Step. Part Two

Slightly Off Ground

R

L

L

R

Fig. 88.

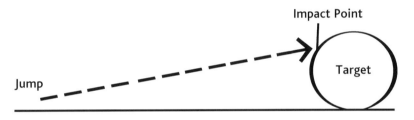

Impact Point

Target

Jump

Fig. 89.

Turn right hip and right side of torso toward opponent to a right linear position.

Throw right arm behind right leg during the strike for added momentum.
Roll right shoulder into right side of face for coverage of right cheek and chin.

Move left arm to the right across centerline against right cheek for further coverage of right cheek and chin. (Fig. 90)

The strike will move in a direct line to target.

Strike with kneecap.

Land on left leg.

Return to Muay Thai stance facing opponent.

Fig. 90.

UPPER BODY DEFENSES

PARRY (LEFT)

PARRY (RIGHT)

COVER HIGH (LEFT)

COVER HIGH (RIGHT)

COVER LOW OUTSIDE (LEFT)

COVER LOW OUTSIDE (RIGHT)

COVER LOW INSIDE (LEFT)

COVER LOW INSIDE (RIGHT)

CUP/CATCH (LEFT)

CUP/CATCH (RIGHT)

SLIP (LEFT)

SLIP (RIGHT)

DUCK

BOB AND WEAVE (LEFT)

BOB AND WEAVE (RIGHT)

SHOULDER STOP (LEFT)

SHOULDER STOP (RIGHT)

STRAIGHT KNEE #1

STRAIGHT KNEE #2

ELBOW JAM (LEFT)

ELBOW JAM (RIGHT)

PUSH (LEFT)

PUSH (RIGHT)

RETREAT AND ADVANCE

BACKWARDS RETREAT

PARRY (LEFT)

The left parry is a quick defense against a cross.

From Muay Thai stance, open left hand and use palm to bump opponent's right cross to the right slightly past centerline.

Drop right hand slightly out of the way of the left parry and turn right shoulder forward against right cheek for coverage of right cheek and chin.

Slightly move head to the left during the parry. (Fig. 91)

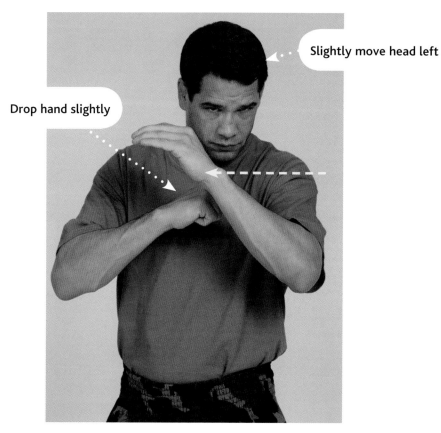

Slightly move head left

Drop hand slightly

Fig. 91.

Do not reach. Wait for opponent's right cross to enter into the range of the parry.

Immediately return to Muay Thai stance.

The left parry can be done from any direction of movement depending on distance and positioning with opponent.

PARRY (RIGHT)

The right parry is a quick defense against a jab.

From Muay Thai stance, open right hand and use palm to bump opponent's jab to the left slightly past centerline.

Drop left hand slightly out of the way of the right parry and turn left shoulder forward against left cheek for coverage of left cheek and chin.

Slightly move head to the right during the parry. (Fig. 92)

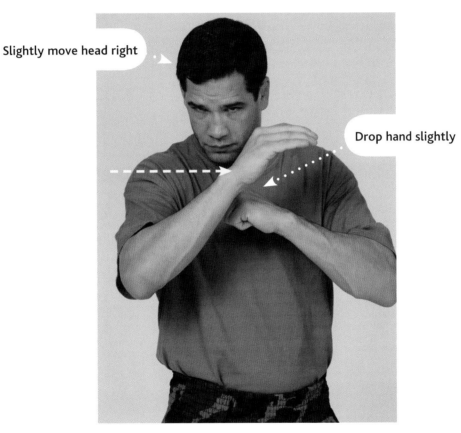

Fig. 92.

Do not reach. Wait for opponent's jab to enter into the range of the parry.

Immediately return to Muay Thai stance.

The right parry can be done from any direction of movement depending on distance and positioning with opponent.

COVER HIGH (LEFT)

The left cover high is a defense against high attacks to the center and left side of the head.

From Muay Thai stance, lift left elbow up to eye-level and slightly to the right, lining up point of left elbow on centerline.

Keep left arm in tight contact with left side of head.

Cover left ear with left fist.

Move right fist against right cheek for coverage of right cheek and chin. (Fig. 93)

Move lateral right during the cover to reduce the impact of the strike.

After the impact, return to Muay Thai stance.

The left cover high can be used to defend against opponent's cross, right hook, right horizontal elbow, right down elbow, right up elbow, high right round kick, high right angle kick, and high short foot jab.

The left cover high also can be done from a stationary stance or any direction of movement depending on distance and positioning with opponent.

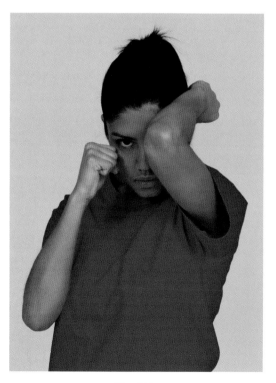

Fig. 93.

COVER HIGH (RIGHT)

The right cover high is a defense against high attacks to the center and right side of the head.

From Muay Thai stance, lift right elbow up to eye-level and slightly to the left, lining up point of right elbow on centerline.

Keep right arm in tight contact with right side of head.

Cover right ear with right fist.

Move left fist against left cheek for coverage of left cheek and chin. (Fig. 94)

Move lateral left during the cover to reduce the impact of the strike.
After the impact, return to Muay Thai stance.

The right cover high can be used to defend against opponent's jab, left hook, left horizontal elbow, left down elbow, left up elbow, high left round kick, high left angle kick, and high long foot jab.

The right cover high also can be done from a stationary stance or any direction of movement depending on distance and positioning with opponent.

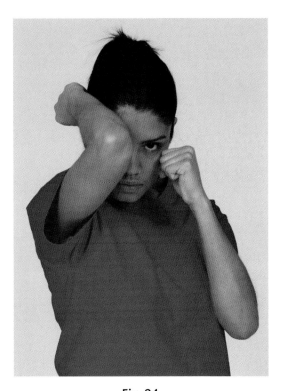

Fig. 94.

COVER LOW OUTSIDE (LEFT)

The left cover low outside is a defense against attacks to the left side of the torso.

From Muay Thai stance, tilt upper body to the left by "crunching" left side of torso.

Move left elbow in tight against left side of torso.

Keep fists at eye-level and move against cheeks for coverage of cheeks and chin. (Fig. 95)

Move lateral right during the cover to reduce the impact of the strike.

After the impact, return to Muay Thai stance.

The left cover low outside can be used to defend against opponent's right low hook, mid-right round kick, and mid-right angle kick.

The left cover low outside also can be done from a stationary stance or any direction of movement depending on distance and positioning with opponent.

Fig. 95.

COVER LOW OUTSIDE (RIGHT)

The right cover low outside is a defense against attacks to the right side of the torso.

From Muay Thai stance, tilt upper body to the right by "crunching" right side of torso.

Move right elbow in tight against right side of torso.

Keep fists at eye-level and move against cheeks for coverage of cheeks and chin. (Fig. 96)

Move lateral left during the cover to reduce the impact of the strike.

After the impact, return to Muay Thai stance.

The right cover low outside can be used to defend against opponent's left low hook, mid-left round kick, and mid-left angle kick.

The right cover low outside also can be done from a stationary stance or any direction of movement depending on distance and positioning with opponent.

Fig. 96.

COVER LOW INSIDE (LEFT)

The left cover low inside is a defense against attacks to the front midsection.

From Muay Thai stance, move left elbow to the right and align fist and elbow vertical on centerline. Rotate left fist so palm is facing you. Move right hand against right cheek for coverage of right cheek and chin.

"Crunch" midsection. Move left shoulder forward and drop slightly.

Keep left elbow tight against your body.

Keep both fists at eye-level. (Fig. 97)

Retreat during the cover to reduce the impact of the strike.

After the impact, return to Muay Thai stance.

The left cover low inside can be used to defend against opponent's low cross, long foot jab, short foot jab, left long knee, and right long knee.

The left cover low inside also can be done from a stationary stance or any direction of movement depending on distance and positioning with opponent.

Fig. 97.

COVER LOW INSIDE (RIGHT)

The right cover low inside is a defense against attacks to the front midsection.

From Muay Thai stance, move right elbow to the left and align fist and elbow vertical on centerline. Rotate right fist so palm is facing you. Move left hand against left cheek for coverage of left cheek and chin.

"Crunch" midsection. Move right shoulder forward and drop slightly.

Keep right elbow tight against your body.

Keep both fists at eye-level. (Fig. 98)

Retreat during the cover to reduce the impact of the strike.

After the impact, return to Muay Thai stance.

The right cover low inside can be used to defend against opponent's low jab, long foot jab, short foot jab, left long knee, and right long knee.

The right cover low inside also can be done from a stationary stance or any direction of movement depending on distance and positioning with opponent.

Fig. 98.

CUP/CATCH (LEFT)

The left cup/catch is a defense against the jab or cross and can be altered as a defense against uppercuts.

From Muay Thai stance, open left fist and rotate palm away, slightly "cupping" hand.

Move left palm slightly forward on centerline in front of face to slap the strike and absorb the impact.

Do not grab.

Do not reach. Wait for opponent's cross or jab to enter into the range of the cup/catch.

Keep both hands at eye-level.

Right arm stays in original position. (Fig. 99)

Fig. 99.

Retreat during the cup/catch to reduce the impact of the strike.

After the impact, return to Muay Thai stance.

Fig. 100.

The left cup catch also can be altered as a defense against opponent's right uppercut. From Muay Thai stance, rotate left arm horizontal to the right. During rotation, open left fist with palm facing down and slightly "cup" hand. Slap the strike to absorb the impact below chin on centerline. Do not drop elbows. Do not rotate hand. (Fig. 100)

The left cup/catch can be also done from a stationary stance or any direction of movement depending on distance and positioning with opponent.

CUP/CATCH (RIGHT)

The right cup/catch is a defense against the jab or cross and can be altered as a defense against uppercuts.

From Muay Thai stance, open right fist and rotate palm away, slightly "cupping" hand.

Move right palm slightly forward on centerline in front of face to slap the strike and absorb the impact.

Do not grab.

Do not reach. Wait for opponent's cross or jab to enter into the range of the cup/catch.

Keep both hands at eye-level.

Left arm stays in original position. (Fig. 101)

Retreat during the cup/catch to reduce the impact of the strike.

After the impact, return to Muay Thai stance.

The right cup catch also can be altered as a defense against an opponent's left uppercut. From Muay Thai stance, rotate right arm horizontal to the left. During rotation, open right fist with palm facing down and slightly "cup" hand. Slap the strike to absorb the impact below chin on centerline. Do not drop elbows. Do not rotate hand. (Fig. 102)

The right cup/catch also can be done from a stationary stance or any direction of movement depending on distance and positioning with opponent.

Fig. 101.

Fig. 102.

SLIP (LEFT)

The left slip is a defense against the jab or cross.

From Muay Thai stance, step left lead leg forward and to the left in a diagonal line close to opponent. Drop 80% of weight on left lead leg and bend both knees during step to drop eye-level. Right leg will follow. (Fig. 103)

Move head to the left slightly off centerline so opponent's strike grazes off right side of forehead.

Move right shoulder slightly forward during the step and move right elbow in tight against the body.

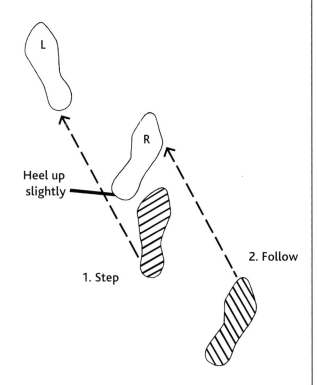

Fig. 103.

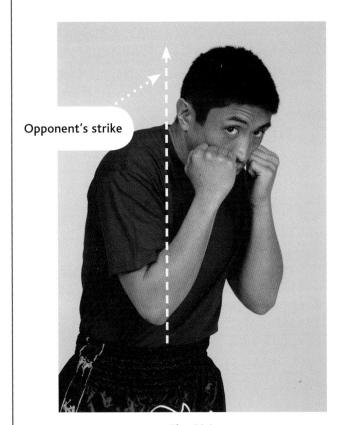

Fig. 104.

Keep both fists at eye-level and move against cheeks for coverage of cheeks and chin. (Fig. 104)

After the slip, you have the option of striking or returning to Muay Thai stance, depending on distance and positioning with opponent.

The direction of the slip depends on desired positioning to opponent.

The left slip also can be done from a stationary stance, forward advance movement, or left lateral movement depending on desired distance and positioning with opponent.

SLIP (RIGHT)

The right slip is a defense against the jab or cross.

From Muay Thai stance, step right rear leg one full step forward and to the right in a diagonal line close to opponent. Drop 80% of weight on right leg and bend both knees during step to drop eye-level. Left leg will follow and return to left lead position facing opponent. (Fig. 105)

Move head to the right slightly off centerline so opponent's strike grazes off left side of forehead.

Move left shoulder slightly forward during the step and move left elbow in tight against the body. Keep both fists at eye-level and move against cheeks for coverage of cheeks and chin. (Fig. 106)

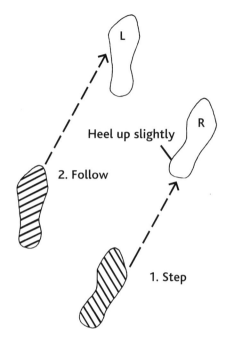

Heel up slightly

2. Follow

L

R

1. Step

Fig. 105.

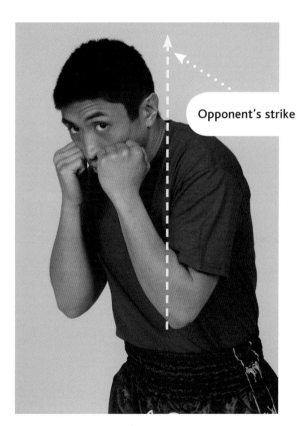

Opponent's strike

Fig. 106.

After the slip, you have the option of striking or returning to Muay Thai stance, depending on distance and positioning with opponent.

The direction of the slip depends on desired positioning to opponent.

The right slip also can be done from a stationary stance, forward advance movement, or right lateral movement depending on desired distance and positioning with opponent.

DUCK

The duck is a defense against most attacks to the head.

From Muay Thai stance, drop eye-level by bending both knees substantially.

Both arms will move in and make tight contact with each other on centerline.

Rotate fists so palms face you.

Both fists are eye-level for coverage of cheeks and chin.

"Crunch" midsection to allow more coverage from elbows. (Fig. 107)

Return to Muay Thai stance.

The duck can be used to defend against opponent's jab, cross, left hook, right hook, left horizontal elbow, right horizontal elbow, high right round kick, and high left round kick.

The duck also can be done from a retreat or advance movement depending on distance and positioning with opponent.

Drop on centerline

Fig. 107.

BOB AND WEAVE (LEFT)

The left bob and weave is a defense against high attacks to the center and left side of the head.

From Muay Thai stance, move both arms in and make tight contact with the body and each other on centerline.

Rotate fists so palms face you and make tight contact with cheeks.

Both fists are eye-level for coverage of cheeks and chin.

Drop eye-level by bending both knees substantially.

Dip upper body from waist up and move to the left creating an arc motion slightly under the incoming strike. (Fig. 108)

Do not step.

"Crunch" midsection at lowest point of arc to allow more coverage from elbows.

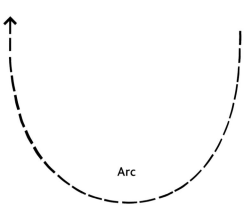

Arc

Facing opponent

Fig. 108.

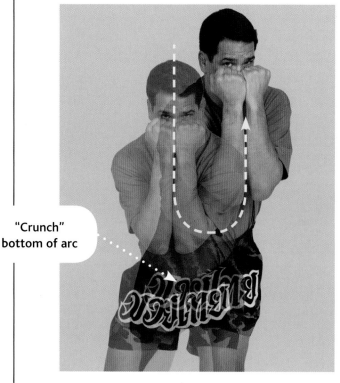

"Crunch" bottom of arc

Fig. 109.

Stand back up to original eye-level. (Fig. 109)

Return to Muay Thai stance.

The left bob and weave can be used to defend against opponent's jab, cross, right hook, and right horizontal elbow.

The left bob and weave can also be done from an advance or left lateral movement depending on distance and positioning with opponent.

BOB AND WEAVE (RIGHT)

The right bob and weave is a defense against high attacks to the center and right side of the head.

From Muay Thai stance, move both arms in and make tight contact with the body and each other on centerline.

Rotate fists so palms face you and make tight contact with cheeks.

Both fists are eye-level for coverage of cheeks and chin.

Drop eye-level by bending both knees substantially.

Dip upper body from waist up and move to the right creating an arc motion slightly under the incoming strike. (Fig. 110)

Do not step.

"Crunch" midsection at lowest point of arc to allow more coverage from elbows.

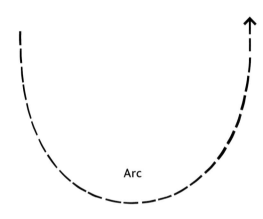

Arc

Facing opponent

Fig. 110.

Stand back up to original eye-level. (Fig. 111)

Return to Muay Thai stance.

The right bob and weave can be used to defend against opponent's jab, cross, left hook, and left horizontal elbow.

The right bob and weave can also be done from an advance or right lateral movement depending on distance and positioning with opponent.

"Crunch" bottom of arc

Fig. 111.

SHOULDER STOP (LEFT)

The left shoulder stop is a defense against the cross and right hook.

From Muay Thai stance, open left fist with palm toward opponent, slightly "cup" left hand and shoot quickly at eye-level in a direct line to opponent's right shoulder.

Roll left shoulder forward into left side of face for coverage of left cheek and chin.

Move right fist against right cheek for coverage of right cheek and chin. (Fig. 112)

Fig. 112.

Return to Muay Thai stance.

The left shoulder stop is used to disrupt opponent's cross or right hook by stopping opponent's right shoulder from moving forward during the strike.

Do not grab.

The left shoulder stop can also be done from any direction of movement depending on distance and positioning with opponent.

SHOULDER STOP (RIGHT)

The right shoulder stop is a defense against the left hook.

From Muay Thai stance, open right fist with palm toward opponent, slightly "cup" right hand and shoot quickly at eye-level in a direct line to opponent's left shoulder.

Roll right shoulder forward into right side of face for coverage of right cheek and chin.

Move left fist against left cheek for coverage of left cheek and chin. (Fig. 113)

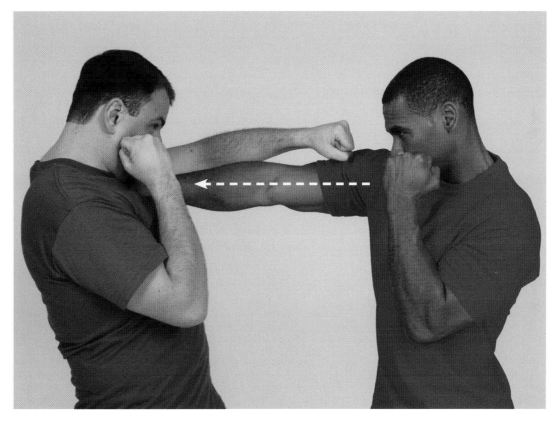

Fig. 113.

Return to Muay Thai stance.

The right shoulder stop is used to disrupt opponent's left hook by stopping opponent's left shoulder from moving forward during the strike.

Do not grab.

The right shoulder stop also can be done from any direction of movement depending on distance and positioning with opponent.

STRAIGHT KNEE #1

The straight knee #1 is a defense used in reaction to an opponent's **unexpected** right cross and includes a follow-up strike.

From Muay Thai stance, lean forward and shift 100% of weight to left lead leg.

Throw left arm straight forward at eye-level, open left fist and "cup" hand. Bend left elbow to swipe opponent's cross to the right off centerline by swiping outside of opponent's arm.

Right hand shoots immediately over left arm and from the outside of opponent's right arm straight forward to opponent's right shoulder. Open and "cup" right hand. (Fig. 114)

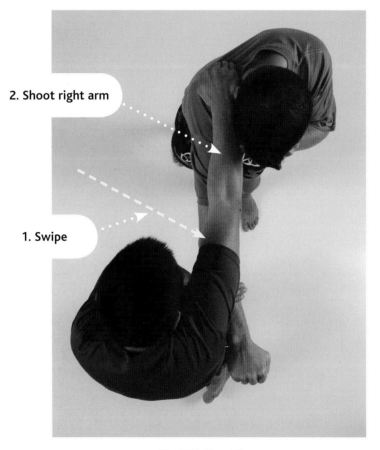

Fig. 114. Top View

From this position, pull opponent into the strike with a quick bump to opponent's right shoulder using right arm.

Do not grab, only cup right hand and bump opponent toward you during the strike.

Lift and bend right knee while quickly thrusting it forward directly at target.

Right foot will point toes down.

Left foot will raise left heel during the strike and be completely on ball of left foot.

Do not pivot. (Fig. 115)

Bump opponent into strike

Raise heel

Fig. 115.

Keep both elbows at eye-level during the strike.

The strike will move in a direct line to target.

Strike with kneecap.

After the strike, place right leg behind you in Muay Thai stance.

STRAIGHT KNEE #2

The straight knee #2 is a defense against opponent's right cross and includes a follow-up strike.

From Muay Thai stance, use both arms to swipe opponent's cross to the right off centerline by swiping outside of opponent's entire arm down toward your right hip. Open both fists and "cup" hands.

Do not grab.

Use the swiping of opponent's entire arm to keep opponent's forward momentum and draw opponent into the strike. (Fig. 116)

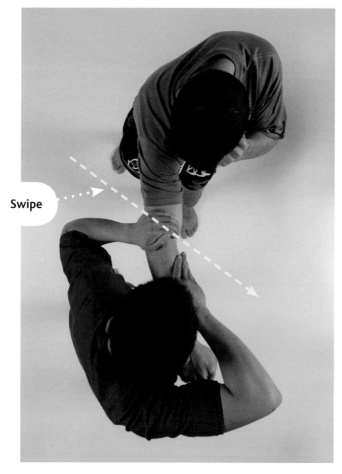

Swipe

Fig. 116. Top View

Shift 100% of weight to left lead leg.

Lift and bend right knee while quickly thrusting it forward directly at target.

Right foot will point toes down.

Left foot will raise left heel during the strike and be completely on ball of left foot.

Do not pivot. (Fig. 117)

Raise heel

Fig. 117.

The strike will move in a direct line to target.

Strike with kneecap.

After the strike, place right leg behind you in Muay Thai stance.

ELBOW JAM (LEFT)

The left elbow jam is a defense against opponent's right horizontal, right down, and right up elbow.

From Muay Thai stance, move left forearm forward, keeping left elbow bent and not dropping the level. Left forearm will make contact with opponent's right forearm during opponent's strike. Slide up opponent's right forearm in a direct line to opponent's right shoulder and chest. Open left fist with palm toward opponent and "cup" left hand. Left forearm will end up flush against opponent's right shoulder and chest.

Roll left shoulder forward into left side of face for coverage of left cheek and chin.

Move right fist against right cheek for coverage of right cheek and chin. (Fig. 118-119)

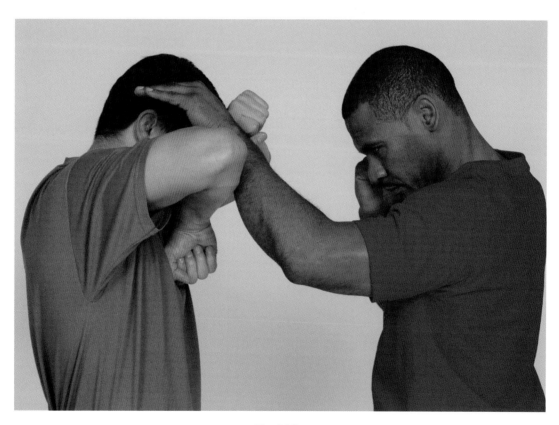

Fig. 118.

For opponent's right down elbow, you may have to adjust the left arm to make initial contact with opponent's forearm.

After the left elbow jam, you have the option to strike from the new distance and position, go into a plum/clinch or return to Muay Thai stance.

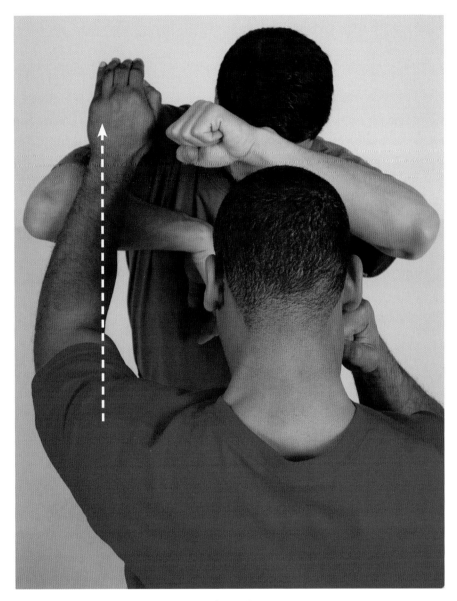

Fig. 119.

The left elbow jam is used to disrupt opponent's right elbow by blocking the line of attack and stopping opponent's right elbow from moving forward during the strike.

Do not grab.

The left elbow jam also can be done from any direction of movement depending on distance and positioning with opponent.

ELBOW JAM (RIGHT)

The right elbow jam is a defense against opponent's left horizontal, left down, and left up elbow.

From Muay Thai stance, move right forearm forward, keeping right elbow bent and not dropping the level. Right forearm will make contact with opponent's left forearm during opponent's strike. Slide up opponent's left forearm in a direct line to opponent's left shoulder and chest. Open right fist with palm toward opponent and "cup" right hand. Right forearm will end up flush against opponent's left shoulder and chest.

Roll right shoulder forward into right side of face for coverage of right cheek and chin.

Move left fist against left cheek for coverage of left cheek and chin. (Fig. 120-121)

Fig. 120.

For opponent's left down elbow, you may have to adjust the right arm to make initial contact with opponent's forearm.

After the right elbow jam, you have the option to strike from the new distance and position, go into a plum/clinch or return to Muay Thai stance.

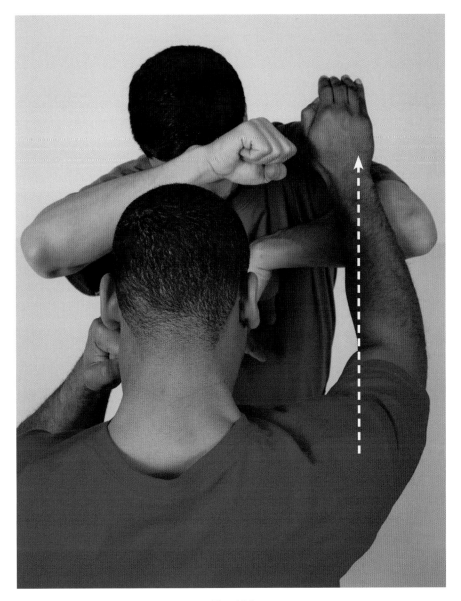

Fig. 121.

The right elbow jam is used to disrupt opponent's left elbow by blocking the line of attack and stopping opponent's left elbow from moving forward during the strike.

Do not grab.

The right elbow jam also can be done from any direction of movement depending on distance and positioning with opponent.

PUSH (LEFT)

The left push is used to create distance and disrupt opponent's strikes.

From Muay Thai stance, open left fist with palm toward opponent and "cup" left hand. Thrust hand at eye-level in a direct line to opponent's chest and push opponent backwards using left palm.

Roll left shoulder forward into left side of face for coverage of left cheek and chin.

Move right fist against right cheek for coverage of right cheek and chin. (Fig. 122)

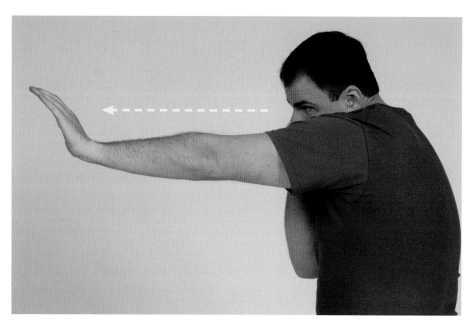

Fig. 122.

Move right leg one step forward and to the right. Drop 80% of weight onto right leg and use the step for added momentum.

Return to Muay Thai stance.

The left push is used to create distance, stop opponent's forward momentum, and disrupt opponent's technique by pushing off balance.

Do not grab.

The left push can be used to defend against opponent's cross, right hook, right horizontal elbow, right down elbow, right up elbow, and high or mid-right round kick.

The left push also can be done from any direction of movement depending on distance and positioning with opponent.

PUSH (RIGHT)

The right push is used to create distance and disrupt opponent's strikes.

From Muay Thai stance, open right fist with palm toward opponent and "cup" right hand. Thrust hand at eye-level in a direct line to opponent's chest and push opponent backwards using right palm.

Roll right shoulder forward into right side of face for coverage of right cheek and chin.

Move left fist against left cheek for coverage of left cheek and chin. (Fig. 123)

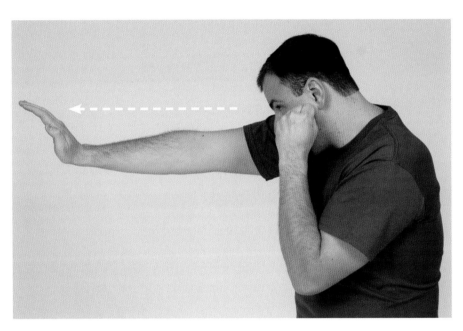

Fig. 123.

Move left leg one step forward and to the left. Drop 80% of weight onto left leg and use the step for added momentum.

Return to Muay Thai stance.

The right push is used to create distance, stop opponent's forward momentum, and disrupt opponent's technique by pushing off balance.

Do not grab.

The right push can be used to defend against opponent's left hook, left horizontal elbow, left down elbow, left up elbow, and high or mid-left round kick.

The right push also can be done from any direction of movement depending on distance and positioning with opponent.

RETREAT AND ADVANCE

The retreat and advance is a defense against upper body strikes.

The retreat and advance is a combination of two movements: the backwards retreat and the forward advance.

From Muay Thai stance, retreat out of opponent's strike range by quickly stepping backwards with right rear leg and pushing backwards with left lead leg. Left lead leg will follow to Muay Thai stance.

After full extension of opponent's strike, immediately step forward with left lead leg and push forward with right rear leg. Right rear leg will follow and end in Muay Thai stance.

The retreat and advance can be used to defend against any upper body strike by avoiding the strike and returning to Muay Thai stance at original distance from opponent for a follow-up attack.

BACKWARDS RETREAT

The backwards retreat can be used as a defense against upper body strikes.

From Muay Thai stance, retreat out of opponent's strike range by quickly stepping backwards with right rear leg and pushing backwards with left lead leg. Left lead leg will follow and end in Muay Thai stance.

The backwards retreat can be used to defend against any upper body strike by avoiding the strike.

  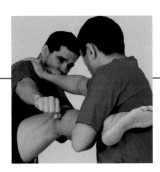

LOWER BODY DEFENSES

LEAD LEG SHIELD

The lead leg shield is a defense against opponent's mid or low kicks.

From Muay Thai stance, move left and right fist against both cheeks for coverage of cheeks and chin. Angle left elbow out slightly to the left away from the body. "Crunch" midsection to lower the level of both elbows.

Shift 100% of weight to right leg. Right foot will be flatfooted.

Bend left knee, lift left leg up and angle shin out slightly to the left toward opponent's kick. Raise knee to meet with inside of left elbow.

Angle left foot up to flex and tighten muscles around shin area. (Fig. 124)

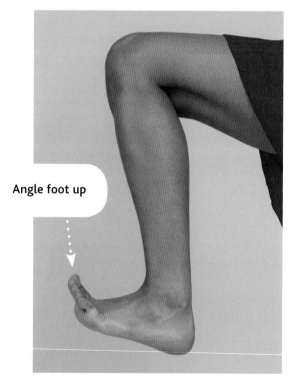

Angle foot up

Fig. 124.

Maintain balance with right leg.

Take the impact from the strike on shin area of left leg. (Fig. 125)

After the impact, set left leg down in original position and return to Muay Thai stance.

You can adjust the angle and level of the shield to ensure contact with the strike on the shin area.

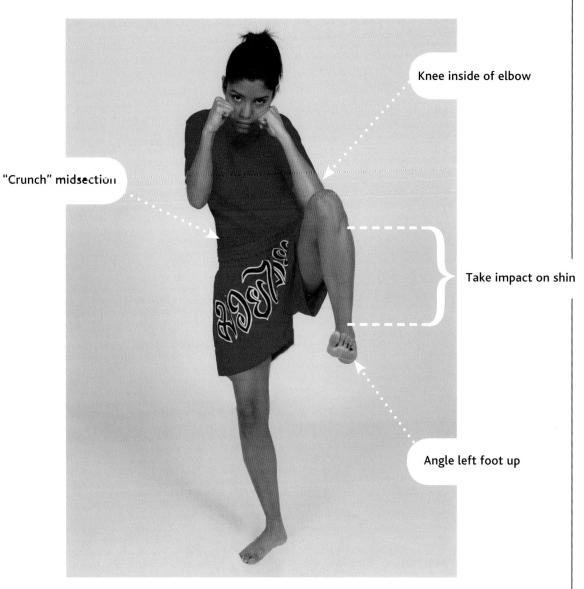

Knee inside of elbow

"Crunch" midsection

Take impact on shin

Angle left foot up

Fig. 125.

The lead leg shield is used to block mid or low kicks to your left side and keep your position/distance with opponent.

The lead leg shield can be used to defend against opponent's mid or low right round kick, mid or low right angle kick, and right cut kick.

The lead leg shield also can be done from a retreat or right linear movement depending on distance and positioning with opponent.

CROSS SHIELD

The cross shield is a defense against opponent's mid-level or low level left round kick.

From Muay Thai stance, move left and right fist against both cheeks for coverage of cheeks and chin and "crunch" midsection to lower the level of both elbows.

Shift 100% of weight to right leg. Right foot will be flatfooted.

Bend left knee, lift left leg up and move it to the right across the body. Knee will meet with inside of right elbow. Angle left shin out.

Angle left foot up to flex and tighten muscles around shin area. (Fig. 126)

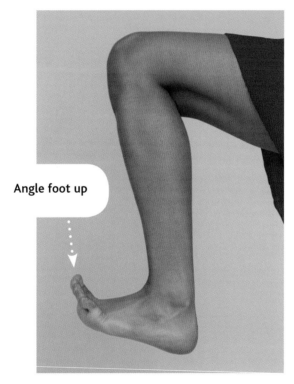

Angle foot up

Fig. 126.

Maintain balance with right leg.

Take the impact from the strike on shin area of left leg. (Fig. 127)

After the impact, set left leg down in original position and return to Muay Thai stance.

You can adjust the angle and level of the shield to ensure contact with the strike on the shin area.

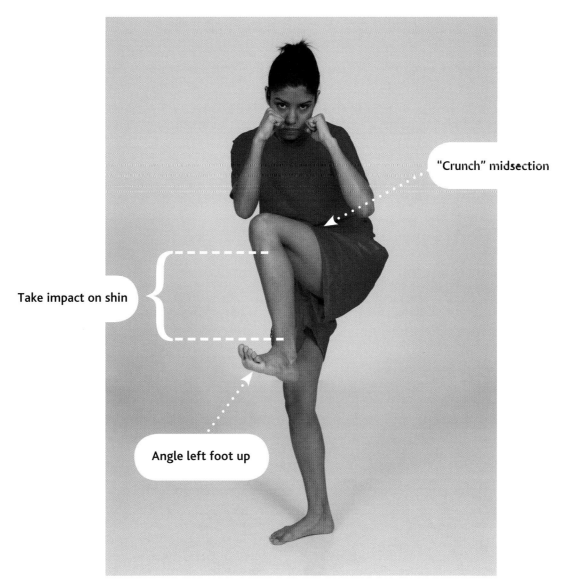

Fig. 127.

The cross shield is used to block mid or low kicks to your right side and keep your position/distance with opponent.

The cross shield can be used to defend against opponent's mid or low left round kick, mid or low left angle kick, and left cut kick.

The cross shield also can be done from a retreat or right linear movement depending on distance and positioning with opponent.

SWEEP/PARRY LEFT ROUND KICK

The sweep/parry left round kick is a defense against opponent's mid-left round kick.

From Muay Thai stance, retreat out of range by quickly stepping backwards with right rear leg and pushing backwards with left lead leg. Left lead leg will follow.

Open left fist, "cup" hand, and with left arm, make a circular motion clockwise behind opponent's left kick. Keep left elbow at original level throughout the technique. Left hand will make contact **behind** opponent's left kick. Once left hand makes contact, cup/hook hand and pass opponent's left kick to the left past your body and return left arm to original position.

Do not grab.

Do not reach. Wait for the strike to come into the range of the sweep/parry.

During the sweep/parry, move right fist against right cheek for coverage of right cheek and chin. Move right elbow in tight against the body for coverage of right torso. (Fig. 128)

After opponent's left kick is past the body, immediately step forward with left lead leg and push forward with right rear leg. Right rear leg will follow.

Return to Muay Thai stance with original distance from opponent.

Cup hand

Fig. 128.

SWEEP/PARRY RIGHT ROUND KICK

The sweep/parry right round kick is a defense against opponent's mid-right round kick.

From Muay Thai stance, retreat out of range by quickly stepping backwards with right rear leg and pushing backwards with left lead leg. Left lead leg will follow.

Open right fist, "cup" hand and with right arm, make a circular motion counter-clockwise behind opponent's right kick. Keep right elbow at original level throughout the technique. Right hand will make contact **behind** opponent's right kick. Once right hand makes contact, cup/hook hand and pass opponent's right kick to the right past your body and return right arm to original position.

Do not grab.

Do not reach. Wait for the strike to come into the range of the sweep/parry.

During the sweep/parry, move left fist against left cheek for coverage of left cheek and chin. Move left elbow in tight against the body for coverage of left torso. (Fig. 129)

After opponent's right kick is past the body, immediately step forward with left lead leg and push forward with right rear leg. Right rear leg will follow.

Return to Muay Thai stance with original distance from opponent.

Cup hand

Fig. 129.

PARRY LONG FOOT JAB INSIDE

The parry long foot jab inside is a defense against opponent's long foot jab.

From Muay Thai stance, move right lateral by stepping directly to the right with right rear leg and pushing to the right with left lead leg. Left lead leg will follow.

Open left fist, "cup" hand, and with left arm, make a circular motion clockwise. Keep left elbow at original level throughout the technique. Left hand or forearm will make contact to the **outside** of opponent's long foot jab (the left side of opponent's left leg). Once left hand or forearm makes contact, cup/hook hand and pass opponent's long foot jab to the left past your body and return left arm to original position.

Do not grab.

Do not reach. Wait for the strike to come into the range of the parry.

During the parry, move right fist against right cheek for coverage of right cheek and chin. Move right elbow in tight against the body for coverage of right torso. (Fig. 130)

During the parry, you may twist the upper body to a right linear position, if needed (to avoid opponent's foot jab making contact with the body). After the pass, immediately square off upper body.

Return to Muay Thai stance.

The parry long foot jab inside allows you to defend against the long foot jab and position yourself to the outside of opponent.

The parry long foot jab inside also can be done from a retreat or retreat and advance movement depending on distance and positioning with opponent.

Cup hand

Fig. 130.

PARRY LONG FOOT JAB OUTSIDE

The parry long foot jab outside is a defense against opponent's long foot jab.

From Muay Thai stance, move left lateral by stepping directly to the left with left lead leg and pushing to the left with right rear leg. Right rear leg will follow.

Open right fist, "cup" hand, and with right arm, make a circular motion counter-clockwise. Keep right elbow at original level throughout the technique. Right hand or forearm will make contact to the **inside** of opponent's long foot jab (the right side of opponent's left leg). Once right hand or forearm makes contact, cup/hook hand and pass opponent's long foot jab to the right past your body and return right arm to original position.

Do not grab.

Do not reach. Wait for the strike to come into the range of the parry.

During the parry, move left fist against left cheek for coverage of left cheek and chin. Move left elbow in tight against the body for coverage of left torso. (Fig. 131)

During the parry, you may twist the upper body to a left linear position, if needed (to avoid opponent's foot jab making contact with the body). After the pass, immediately square off upper body.

Return to Muay Thai stance.

The parry long foot jab outside allows you to defend against the long foot jab and position yourself to the inside of opponent.

The parry long foot jab outside also can be done from a retreat or retreat and advance movement depending on distance and positioning with opponent.

Cup hand

Fig. 131.

PARRY SHORT FOOT JAB INSIDE

The parry short foot jab inside is a defense against opponent's short foot jab.

From Muay Thai stance, move left lateral by stepping directly to the left with left lead leg and pushing to the left with right rear leg. Right rear leg will follow.

Open right fist, "cup" hand, and with right arm, make a circular motion counter-clockwise. Keep right elbow at original level throughout the technique. Right hand or forearm will make contact to the **outside** of opponent's short foot jab (the right side of opponent's right leg). Once right hand or forearm makes contact, cup/hook hand and pass opponent's short foot jab to the right past your body and return right arm to original position.

Do not grab.

Do not reach. Wait for the strike to come into the range of the parry.

During the parry, move left fist against left cheek for coverage of left cheek and chin. Move left elbow in tight against the body for coverage of left torso. (Fig. 132)

During the parry, you may twist the upper body to a left linear position, if needed (to avoid opponent's foot jab making contact with the body). After the pass, immediately square off upper body.

Return to Muay Thai stance.

The parry short foot jab inside allows you to defend against the short foot jab and position yourself to the outside of opponent.

The parry short foot jab inside also can be done from a retreat or retreat and advance movement depending on distance and positioning with opponent.

Cup hand

Fig. 132.

PARRY SHORT FOOT JAB OUTSIDE

The parry short foot jab outside is a defense against opponent's short foot jab.

From Muay Thai stance, move right lateral by stepping directly to the right with right rear leg and pushing to the right with left lead leg. Left lead leg will follow.

Open left fist, "cup" hand, and with left arm, make a circular motion clockwise. Keep left elbow at original level throughout the technique. Left hand or forearm will make contact to the **inside** of opponent's short foot jab (the left side of opponent's right leg). Once left hand or forearm makes contact, cup/hook hand and pass opponent's short foot jab to the left past your body and return left arm to original position.

Do not grab.

Do not reach. Wait for the strike to come into the range of the parry.

During the parry, move right fist against right cheek for coverage of right cheek and chin. Move right elbow in tight against the body for coverage of right torso. (Fig. 133)

During the parry, you may twist the upper body to a right linear position, if needed (to avoid opponent's foot jab making contact with the body). After the pass, immediately square off upper body.

Return to Muay Thai stance.

The parry short foot jab outside allows you to defend against the short foot jab and position yourself to the inside of opponent.

The parry short foot jab outside also can be done from a retreat or retreat and advance movement depending on distance and positioning with opponent.

Cup hand

Fig. 133.

PARRY LEFT LONG KNEE INSIDE

The parry left long knee inside is a defense against opponent's left long knee.

From Muay Thai stance, move right lateral by stepping directly to the right with right rear leg and pushing to the right with left lead leg. Left lead leg will follow.

Open left fist, "cup" hand, and with left arm, make a circular motion clockwise. Keep left elbow at original level throughout the technique. Left hand or forearm will make contact to the **outside** of opponent's left knee (the left side of opponent's knee). Once left hand or forearm makes contact, cup/hook hand and pass opponent's left knee to the left past your body and return left arm to original position.

Do not grab.

Do not reach. Wait for the strike to come into the range of the parry.

During the parry, move right fist against right cheek for coverage of right cheek and chin. Move right elbow in tight against the body for coverage of right torso. (Fig. 134)

During the parry, you may twist the upper body to a right linear position, if needed (to avoid opponent's left knee making contact with the body). After the pass, immediately square off upper body.

Return to Muay Thai stance.

The parry left long knee inside allows you to defend against the left long knee and position yourself to the outside of opponent.

The parry left long knee inside also can be done from a retreat or retreat and advance movement depending on distance and positioning with opponent.

Cup hand

Fig. 134.

PARRY LEFT LONG KNEE OUTSIDE

The parry left long knee outside is a defense against opponent's left long knee.

From Muay Thai stance, move left lateral by stepping directly to the left with left lead leg and pushing to the left with right rear leg. Right rear leg will follow.

Open right fist, "cup" hand, and with right arm, make a circular motion counter-clockwise. Keep right elbow at original level throughout the technique. Right hand or forearm will make contact to the **inside** of opponent's left knee (the right side of opponent's left knee). Once right hand or forearm makes contact, cup/hook hand and pass opponent's left knee to the right past your body and return right arm to original position.

Do not grab.

Do not reach. Wait for the strike to come into the range of the parry.

During the parry, move left fist against left cheek for coverage of left cheek and chin. Move left elbow in tight against the body for coverage of left torso. (Fig. 135)

During the parry, you may twist the upper body to a left linear position, if needed (to avoid opponent's left knee making contact with the body). After the pass, immediately square off upper body.

Return to Muay Thai stance.

The parry left long knee outside allows you to defend against the left long knee and position yourself to the inside of opponent.

The parry left long knee outside also can be done from a retreat or retreat and advance movement depending on distance and positioning with opponent.

Cup hand

Fig. 135.

PARRY RIGHT LONG KNEE INSIDE

The parry right long knee inside is a defense against opponent's right long knee.

From Muay Thai stance, move left lateral by stepping directly to the left with left lead leg and pushing to the left with right rear leg. Right rear leg will follow.

Open right fist, "cup" hand, and with right arm, make a circular motion counter-clockwise. Keep right elbow at original level throughout the technique. Right hand or forearm will make contact to the **outside** of opponent's right knee (the right side of opponent's right leg). Once right hand or forearm makes contact, cup/hook hand and pass opponent's right knee to the right past your body and return right arm to original position.

Do not grab.

Do not reach. Wait for the strike to come into the range of the parry.

During the parry, move left fist against left cheek for coverage of left cheek and chin. Move left elbow in tight against the body for coverage of left torso. (Fig. 136)

During the parry, you may twist the upper body to a left linear position, if needed (to avoid opponent's right knee making contact with the body). After the pass, immediately square off upper body.

Return to Muay Thai stance.

The parry right long knee inside allows you to defend against the right long knee and position yourself to the outside of opponent.

The parry right long knee inside also can be done from a retreat or retreat and advance movement depending on distance and positioning with opponent.

Cup hand

Fig. 136.

PARRY RIGHT LONG KNEE OUTSIDE

The parry right long knee outside is a defense against opponent's right long knee.

From Muay Thai stance, move right lateral by stepping directly to the right with right rear leg and pushing to the right with left lead leg. Left lead leg will follow.

Open left fist, "cup" hand, and with left arm, make a circular motion clockwise. Keep left elbow at original level throughout the technique. Left hand or forearm will make contact to the **inside** of opponent's right knee (the left side of opponent's right knee). Once left hand or forearm makes contact, cup/hook hand and pass opponent's right knee to the left past your body and return left arm to original position.

Do not grab.

Do not reach. Wait for the strike to come into the range of the parry.

During the parry, move right fist against right cheek for coverage of right cheek and chin. Move right elbow in tight against the body for coverage of right torso. (Fig. 137)

During the parry, you may twist the upper body to a right linear position, if needed (to avoid opponent's right knee making contact with the body). After the pass, immediately square off upper body.

Return to Muay Thai stance.

The parry right long knee outside allows you to defend against the right long knee and position yourself to the inside of opponent.

The parry right long knee outside also can be done from a retreat or retreat and advance movement depending on distance and positioning with opponent.

Cup hand

Fig. 137.

LEFT ANGLE EVADE KICK

The left angle evade kick is a defense against opponent's left round kick and includes a follow-up strike.

From Muay Thai stance, evade opponent's left round kick by stepping left lead leg forward and to the left at an angle. Right leg will immediately follow the same angle as the left leg and will take the place of left leg (i.e., switch feet in the same spot), dropping 100% of weight to right leg.

Do not place left leg down. (Fig. 138)

Immediately pivot to the right on ball of right foot and left round kick opponent's right leg. Swing left leg forward and align shin horizontal and flush with target.

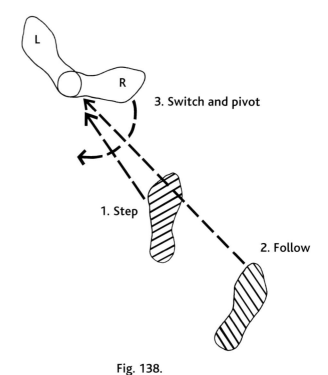

3. Switch and pivot

1. Step

2. Follow

Fig. 138.

Rotate right arm so palm faces out and move to the left across centerline and above eye line. Touch outer forearm across forehead for coverage. Throw left arm behind left leg during the strike for added momentum.

Strike with left shin.

The strike will move from left to right.

After the impact, place left leg behind you and step back with right leg to return to Muay Thai stance at the new distance and position to opponent.

The left angle evade kick allows you to evade opponent's left round kick, strike opponent's right leg (base leg of opponent's left round kick), and position yourself to the outside of opponent.

RIGHT ANGLE EVADE KICK

The right angle evade kick is a defense against opponent's right round kick and includes a follow-up strike.

From Muay Thai stance, evade opponent's right round kick by stepping right rear leg forward and to the right at an angle. Left leg will immediately follow the same angle as right leg and will take the place of right leg (i.e., switch feet in the same spot), dropping 100% of weight to left leg.

Do not place right leg down. (Fig. 139)

Immediately pivot to the left on ball of left foot and right round kick opponent's left leg. Swing right leg forward and align shin horizontal and flush with target.

Rotate left arm so palm faces out and move to the right across centerline and above eye line. Touch outer forearm across forehead for coverage. Throw right arm behind right leg during the strike for added momentum.

Strike with right shin.

The strike will move from right to left.

After the impact, place right leg behind you to return to Muay Thai stance at the new distance and position to opponent.

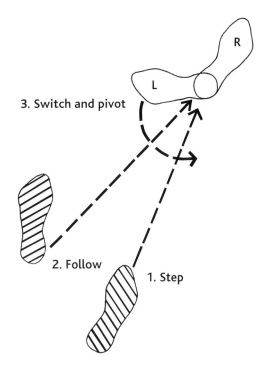

Fig. 139.

The right angle evade kick allows you to evade opponent's right round kick, strike opponent's left leg (base leg of opponent's right round kick), and position yourself to the outside of opponent.

CATCH KICK (LEFT)

The left catch kick is a defense against opponent's mid right round kick or mid right angle kick.

From Muay Thai stance, as opponent throws the right round kick, move right lateral by **completely** moving your entire body past your original centerline, stepping directly to the right with right rear leg and pushing to the right with left lead leg. Left lead leg will follow.

During the right lateral movement, move left arm to the left in a "swooping" motion counter-clockwise over and under opponent's right leg. (Fig. 140)

Trap opponent's right leg around the ankle or lower calf area and lift up to lock it in tight against your body.

Do not grab opponent's leg, only trap it with left arm. Left palm will rest flush against chest. (Fig. 141)

Fig. 140. Facing opponent

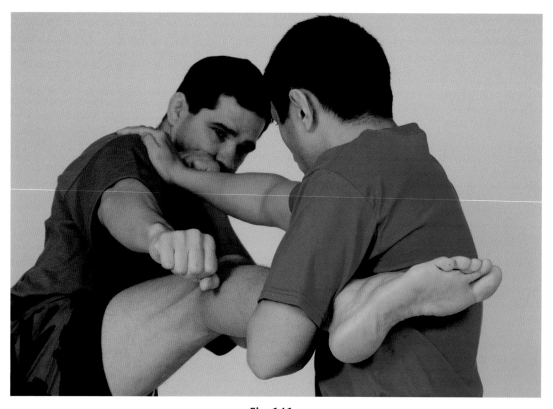

Fig. 141.

Tight against body

Fig. 142.

During the trapping of opponent's right leg, immediately shoot right arm directly towards opponent's right shoulder. Move right shoulder forward into right side of face for coverage. Open right hand with palm toward opponent and push opponent's right shoulder or neck to keep opponent off balance and maintain distance. (Fig. 142)

From the catch kick position, you can sweep opponent, keep opponent off balance, or release the catch kick and follow-up with an attack.

The left catch kick allows you to trap opponent's mid-level right round kick, control opponent's balance, and position opponent for follow-up attacks.

CATCH KICK (RIGHT)

The right catch kick is a defense against opponent's mid left round kick or mid left angle kick.

From Muay Thai stance, as opponent throws the left round kick, move left lateral by **completely** moving your entire body past your original center-line, stepping directly to the left with left lead leg and pushing to the left with right rear leg. Right rear leg will follow.

During the left lateral movement, move right arm to the right in a "swooping" motion clockwise over and under opponent's left leg. (Fig. 143)

Trap opponent's left leg around the ankle or lower calf area and lift up to lock it in tight against your body.

Do not grab the leg only trap it with your right arm. Your right palm will rest flush against your chest. (Fig. 144)

Fig. 143. Facing opponent

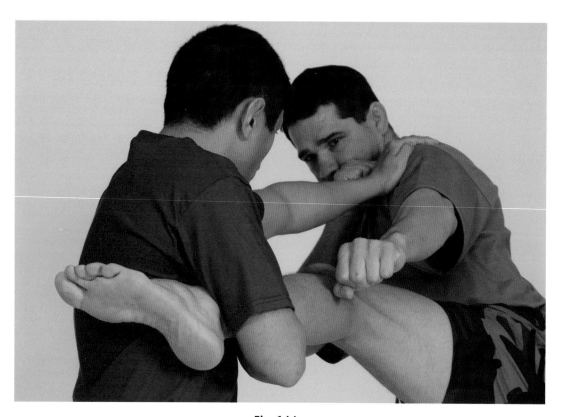

Fig. 144.

Tight against body

Fig. 145.

During the trapping of opponent's left leg, immediately shoot left arm directly towards opponent's left shoulder. Move left shoulder forward into left side of face for coverage. Open left hand with palm toward opponent and push opponent's left shoulder or neck to keep opponent off balance and maintain distance. (Fig. 145)

From the catch kick position, you can sweep opponent, keep opponent off balance, or release the catch kick and follow-up with an attack.

The right catch kick allows you to trap opponent's mid-level left round kick, control opponent's balance, and position opponent for follow-up attacks.

RETREAT AND ADVANCE

The retreat and advance is a defense against lower body strikes.

The retreat and advance is a combination of two movements: the backwards retreat and the forward advance.

From Muay Thai stance, retreat out of opponent's strike range by quickly stepping backwards with right rear leg and pushing backwards with left lead leg. Left lead leg will follow to Muay Thai stance.

After full extension of opponent's strike, immediately step forward with left lead leg and push forward with right rear leg. Right rear leg will follow and end in Muay Thai stance.

The retreat and advance can be used to defend against any lower body strike by avoiding the strike and returning to Muay Thai stance at original distance from opponent for a follow-up attack.

BACKWARDS RETREAT

The backwards retreat can be used as a defense against lower body strikes.

From Muay Thai stance, retreat out of opponent's strike range by quickly stepping backwards with right rear leg and pushing backwards with left lead leg. Left lead leg will follow and end in Muay Thai stance.

The backwards retreat can be used to defend against any lower body strike by avoiding the strike.

STRIKE-
DEFENSE
TABLES

Upper Body Strike-Defense Table

Lower Body Strike-Defense Table

The strike-defense tables are only a standard guide that may be adjusted to fit your needs as your training progresses.

UPPER BODY STRIKE-DEFENSE TABLE

STRIKE	LEVEL	DEFENSE
Jab	High	Parry (Right), Cover High (Right), Cup/Catch (Left), Cup/Catch (Right), Slip (Left), Slip (Right), Duck, Bob and Weave (Left), Bob and Weave (Right), Retreat and Advance, Backwards Retreat
Cross	High	Parry (Left), Cover High (Left), Cup/Catch (Left), Cup/Catch (Right), Slip (Left), Slip (Right), Duck, Bob and Weave (Left), Bob and Weave (Right), Shoulder Stop (Left), Straight Knee #1, Straight Knee #2, Push (Left), Retreat and Advance, Backwards Retreat
Hook (Left)	High	Cover High (Right), Duck, Bob and Weave (Right), Shoulder Stop (Right), Push (Right), Retreat and Advance, Backwards Retreat
Hook (Right)	High	Cover High (Left), Duck, Bob and Weave (Left), Shoulder Stop (Left), Push (Left), Retreat and Advance, Backwards Retreat
Low Jab	Mid	Cover Low Inside (Right), Retreat and Advance, Backwards Retreat
Low Cross	Mid	Cover Low Inside (Left), Retreat and Advance, Backwards Retreat
Low Hook (Left)	Mid	Cover Low Outside (Right), Retreat and Advance, Backwards Retreat
Low Hook (Right)	Mid	Cover Low Outside (Left), Retreat and Advance, Backwards Retreat
Uppercut (Left)	High	Cup/Catch (Left), Cup/Catch (Right), Retreat and Advance, Backwards Retreat
Uppercut (Right)	High	Cup/Catch (Left), Cup/Catch (Right), Retreat and Advance, Backwards Retreat
Horizontal Elbow (Left)	High	Cover High (Right), Duck, Bob and Weave (Right), Elbow Jam (Right), Push (Right), Retreat and Advance, Backwards Retreat
Horizontal Elbow (Right)	High	Cover High (Left), Duck, Bob and Weave (Left), Elbow Jam (Left), Push (Left), Retreat and Advance, Backwards Retreat
Down Elbow (Left)	High	Cover High (Right), Elbow Jam (Right), Push (Right), Retreat and Advance, Backwards Retreat
Down Elbow (Right)	High	Cover High (Left), Elbow Jam (Left), Push (Left), Retreat and Advance, Backwards Retreat

STRIKE	LEVEL	DEFENSE
Up Elbow (Left)	High	Cover High (Right), Elbow Jam (Right), Push (Right), Retreat and Advance, Backwards Retreat
Up Elbow (Right)	High	Cover High (Left), Elbow Jam (Left), Push (Left), Retreat and Advance, Backwards Retreat

When a jump or spin is added to an attack, use the same defenses suggested for that strike but respond according to the distance that is involved.

LOWER BODY STRIKE-DEFENSE TABLE

STRIKE	LEVEL	DEFENSE
Right Round Kick	High	Cover High (Left), Duck, Push (Left), Right Angle Evade Kick, Retreat and Advance, Backwards Retreat
	Mid	Cover Low Outside (Left), Push (Left), Lead Leg Shield, Sweep/ Parry Round Kick (Right), Right Angle Evade Kick, Catch Kick (Left), Retreat and Advance, Backwards Retreat
	Low	Lead Leg Shield, Right Angle Evade Kick, Retreat and Advance, Backwards Retreat
Left Round Kick	High	Cover High (Right), Duck, Push (Right), Left Angle Evade Kick, Retreat and Advance, Backwards Retreat
	Mid	Cover Low Outside (Right), Push (Right), Cross Shield, Sweep/ Parry Round Kick (Left), Left Angle Evade Kick, Catch Kick (Right), Retreat and Advance, Backwards Retreat
	Low	Cross Shield, Left Angle Evade Kick, Retreat and Advance, Backwards Retreat
Angle Kick (Left)	High	Cover High (Right), Retreat and Advance, Backwards Retreat
	Mid	Cover Low Outside (Right), Cross Shield, Catch Kick (Right), Retreat and Advance, Backwards Retreat
	Low	Cross Shield, Retreat and Advance, Backwards Retreat

STRIKE	LEVEL	DEFENSE
Angle Kick (Right)	High	Cover High (Left), Retreat and Advance, Backwards Retreat
	Mid	Cover Low Outside (Left), Lead Leg Shield, Catch Kick (Left), Retreat and Advance, Backwards Retreat
	Low	Lead Leg Shield, Retreat and Advance, Backwards Retreat
Long Foot Jab	High	Cover High (Right), Retreat and Advance, Backwards Retreat
	Mid	Cover Low Inside (Left), Cover Low Inside (Right), Parry Foot Jab Inside (Left), Parry Foot Jab Outside (Right), Retreat and Advance, Backwards Retreat
Short Foot Jab	High	Cover High (Left), Retreat and Advance, Backwards Retreat
	Mid	Cover Low Inside (Left), Cover Low Inside (Right), Parry Foot Jab Inside (Right), Parry Foot Jab Outside (Left), Retreat and Advance, Backwards Retreat
Long Knee (Left)	Mid	Cover Low Inside (Left), Cover Low Inside (Right), Inside Knee Parry (Left), Outside Knee Parry (Right), Retreat and Advance, Backwards Retreat
Long Knee (Right)	Mid	Cover Low Inside (Left), Cover Low Inside (Right), Inside Knee Parry (Right), Outside Knee Parry (Left), Retreat and Advance, Backwards Retreat
Cut Kick (Left)	Low	Cross Shield, Retreat and Advance, Backwards Retreat
Cut Kick (Right)	Low	Lead Leg Shield, Retreat and Advance, Backwards Retreat

When a jump or spin is added to an attack, use the same defenses suggested for that strike but respond according to the distance that is involved.

PLUM/CLINCH

The plum/clinch is a form of standing grappling at close range.

To initiate a plum/clinch from a Muay Thai stance, use the PUMMEL technique (pg. 130–131).

During the plum/clinch, always keep fingers tight together and in a slightly "cupped" position.

PLUM/CLINCH TIE-UPS

DOUBLE HEAD GRAB

HIGH-LOW (LEFT)

HIGH-LOW (RIGHT)

UNDER ARM

DOUBLE HEAD GRAB

The double head grab is a tie-up used to control opponent and defend in the plum/clinch.

Place both hands palm over palm above opponent's neck and on back of opponent's head on round area of opponent's skull. "Cup" back of opponent's head with palms facing you in a palm over palm position.

Do not lock fingers or grab. (Fig. 146)

Arms can be on the inside of opponent's arms for dominant position or to the outside of opponent's arms.

Pull opponent toward you and squeeze elbows together on centerline. Position yourself as close to opponent as possible with no gaps between you and opponent.

Place head against opponent on the right or left side of arms. You can place the front or side of your face against opponent.

Stand up straight and push hips forward against opponent's hips with no gaps between you and opponent.

Fig. 146.

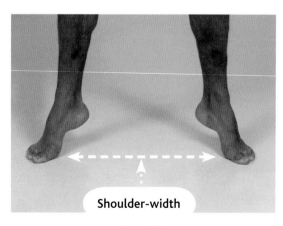

Shoulder-width

Fig. 147.

Place feet shoulder-width apart with both feet pointed out. Distribute weight evenly between both legs. Stay on balls of feet with heels raised. (Fig. 147)

Use arms for forward and backward balance and feet for left and right balance.

From the tie-up, "hang" weight on opponent forcing opponent to deal with the extra weight when opponent maneuvers. (Fig. 148)

Push hips forward

Fig. 148. Double head grab tie-up

HIGH-LOW (LEFT)

The left high-low is a tie-up used to control opponent and defend in the plum/clinch.

Place left hand above opponent's neck and on back of opponent's head on round area of opponent's skull. "Cup" back of opponent's head with palm facing you.

Right hand will be slightly "cupped" and placed on opponent's left hip. Place palm on opponent's left hipbone and relax right arm until desired motion is needed. (Fig. 149)

Palm on opponent's hip

Fig. 149.

Left arm can be on the inside of opponent's arms for dominant position or to the outside of opponent's arms.

Pull opponent toward you and position left elbow on centerline or as close as possible. Position yourself as close to opponent as possible with no gaps between you and opponent.

Place head to the right against opponent. You can place the front or side of your face against opponent.

Stand up straight and push hips forward against opponent's hips with no gaps between you and opponent.

Place feet shoulder-width apart with both feet pointed out. Distribute weight evenly between both legs. Stay on balls of feet with heels raised. (Fig. 150)

Use left arm for forward and backward balance and feet for left and right balance. From tie-up, "hang" weight on opponent forcing opponent to deal with the extra weight when opponent maneuvers. (Fig. 151)

You will need to release your right hand from opponent's hip and lift up when striking with a right curve knee to opponent's left side. After the strike, return right hand to opponent's left hip.

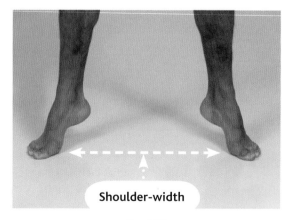

Shoulder-width

Fig. 150.

"Cup" left hand

Fig. 151. Left high-low tie-up (Right hand on opponent's hip)

HIGH-LOW (RIGHT)

The right high-low is a tie-up used to control opponent and defend in the plum/clinch.

Place right hand above opponent's neck and on back of opponent's head on round area of opponent's skull. "Cup" back of opponent's head with palm facing you.

Left hand will be slightly "cupped" and placed on opponent's right hip. Place palm on opponent's right hipbone and relax the left arm until desired motion is needed. (Fig. 152)

"Cup" right hand

Left hand on opponent's hip

Fig. 152.

Right arm can be on the inside of opponent's arms for dominant position or to the outside of opponent's arms.

Pull opponent toward you and position right elbow on centerline or as close as possible. Position yourself as close to opponent as possible with no gaps between you and opponent.

Place head to the left against opponent. You can place the front or side of your face against opponent.

Stand up straight and push hips forward against opponent's hips with no gaps between you and opponent.

Place feet shoulder-width apart with both feet pointed out. Distribute weight evenly between both legs. Stay on balls of feet with heels raised. (Fig. 153)

Use right arm for forward and backward balance and feet for left and right balance.

From the tie-up, "hang" weight on opponent forcing opponent to deal with the extra weight when opponent maneuvers.

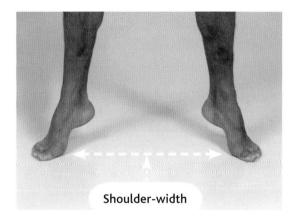

Shoulder-width

Fig. 153.

You will need to release your left hand from opponent's hip and lift up when striking with a left curve knee to opponent's right side. After the strike, return left hand to opponent's right hip.

UNDER ARM

The under arm is a tie-up used to control opponent and defend in the plum/clinch.

Place both arms under opponent's arms as high as possible under opponent's armpits. Grab or clasp hands together behind opponent's back (like a "bear hug").

Do not lock fingers.

Pull opponent toward you and hold tight. Position yourself as close to opponent as possible with no gaps between you and opponent.

Place head against opponent. You can place the front or side of your face against opponent.

Stand up straight and push hips forward against opponent's hips with no gaps between you and opponent. (Fig. 154)

Clasp hands together

Fig. 154. Under arm tie-up

Place feet shoulder-width apart with both feet pointed out. Distribute weight evenly between both legs. Stay on balls of feet with heels raised. (Fig. 155)

Use arms for forward and backward balance and feet for left and right balance.

From the tie-up, "hang" weight on opponent forcing opponent to deal with the extra weight when opponent maneuvers.

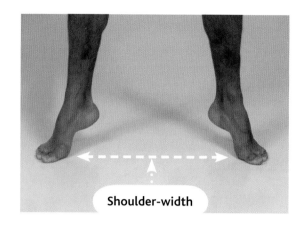

Shoulder-width

Fig. 155.

The under arm tie-up is especially effective against a taller opponent.

  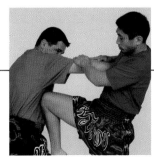

PLUM/CLINCH TIE-UP DEFENSES

PUMMEL (LEFT)

The left pummel is a way to tie-up from a Muay Thai stance, switch tie-ups, or switch to a dominant inside position in the plum/clinch.

Open left hand and "cup" slightly. Shoot left hand through inside of opponent's arms and in a straight line directly past right side of opponent's head. Shoot left hand at eye-level as close to opponent as possible. Roll left shoulder forward against left side of face for coverage. Move right fist against right cheek for coverage. (Fig. 156)

Place left hand above opponent's neck and on back of opponent's head on round area of opponent's skull. "Cup" back of opponent's head with palm facing you.

Shoot left hand directly past opponent's head

*If moving into a double head grab tie-up, continue with right hand immediately opening and shooting through inside of opponent's arms in a straight line directly past the left side of opponent's head. Shoot right hand at eye-level as close to opponent as possible. Roll right shoulder forward and against right side of face for coverage. Place right hand over left hand in a palm over palm position. **Move to entire double head grab tie-up position.***

*If moving into a left high-low tie-up, continue with right hand immediately moving to opponent's left hip. Place palm on opponent's left hipbone and relax right arm until desired motion is needed. **Move to entire left high-low tie-up position.***

Fig. 156.

You can also move into an under arm tie-up by initially shooting the left arm under opponent's right arm as high as possible under opponent's armpit. Follow by shooting right arm under opponent's left armpit and grab or clasp hands together behind opponent's back. **Do not lock fingers.** *Move to entire under arm tie-up position.*

The left pummel can be done from a normal stance to tie-up in plum/clinch, or from an existing tie-up to switch tie-ups or gain inside dominant control.

PUMMEL (RIGHT)

The right pummel is a way to tie-up, switch tie-ups, or switch to a dominant inside position in the plum/clinch.

Open right hand and "cup" slightly. Shoot right hand through inside of opponent's arms and in a straight line directly past left side of opponent's head. Shoot the right hand at eye-level as close to opponent as possible. Roll right shoulder forward against right side of face for coverage. Move left fist against left cheek for coverage. (Fig. 157)

Place right hand above opponent's neck and on back of opponent's head on round area of opponent's skull. "Cup" back of opponent's head with palm facing you.

Shoot right hand directly past opponent's head

Fig. 157.

If moving into a double head grab tie-up, continue with left hand immediately opening and shooting through inside of opponent's arms and in a straight line directly past right side of opponent's head. Shoot left hand at eye-level as close to opponent as possible. Roll left shoulder forward and against left side of face for coverage. Place left hand over right hand in a palm over palm position. **Move to entire double head grab tie-up position.**

If moving into a right high-low tie-up, continue with left hand immediately moving to opponent's right hip. Place palm on opponent's right hipbone and relax left arm until desired motion is needed. **Move to entire right high-low tie-up position.**

You can also move into an under arm tie-up by initially shooting the right arm under opponent's left arm as high as possible under opponent's armpit. Follow by shooting left arm under opponent's right armpit and grab or clasp hands together behind opponent's back. **Do not lock fingers.** *Move to entire under arm tie-up position.*

The right pummel can be done from a normal stance to tie-up in plum/clinch, or from an existing tie-up to switch tie-ups or gain inside dominant control.

CROSS-FACE (LEFT)

The left cross-face is a way to switch tie-ups or switch to a dominant inside position in the plum/clinch.

Open left hand and "cup" slightly. Move left hand from outside of opponent's right arm over and to the right to opponent's right side of chin. Place left palm on opponent's right side of chin and push to the right past centerline turning opponent's face away and to the right, creating space. (Fig. 158)

Keep contact with left hand and pummel in with right hand through inside of opponent's arms. Place right hand above opponent's neck and on back of opponent's head on round area of opponent's skull. "Cup" back of opponent's head with palm facing you.

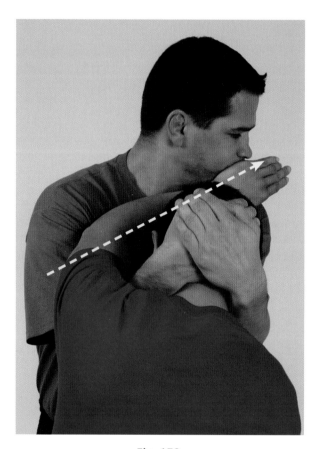

Fig. 158.

If moving into a double head grab tie-up, continue by releasing left hand and immediately shoot left hand through inside of opponent's arms and in a straight line directly past right side of opponent's head. Shoot left hand at eye-level as close to opponent as possible. Roll left shoulder forward and against left side of face for coverage. Place left hand over right hand in a palm over palm position. **Move to entire double head grab tie-up position.**

If moving into a right high-low tie-up, continue by releasing left hand and immediately move left hand to opponent's right hip. Place palm on opponent's right hipbone and relax left arm until desired motion is needed. **Move to entire right high-low tie-up position.**

You can also move into an under arm tie-up by initially shooting the right arm under opponent's left arm as high as possible under opponent's armpit. Follow by shooting left arm under opponent's right armpit and grab or clasp hands together behind opponent's back. **Do not lock fingers.** *Move to entire under arm tie-up position.*

The left cross-face can be done from an existing tie-up to switch tie-ups or gain inside dominant control.

CROSS-FACE (RIGHT)

The right cross-face is a way to switch tie-ups or switch to a dominant inside position in the plum/clinch.

Open right hand and "cup" slightly. Move right hand from outside of opponent's left arm over and to the left to opponent's left side of chin. Place right palm on opponent's left side of chin and push to the left past centerline turning opponent's face away and to the left, creating space. (Fig. 159)

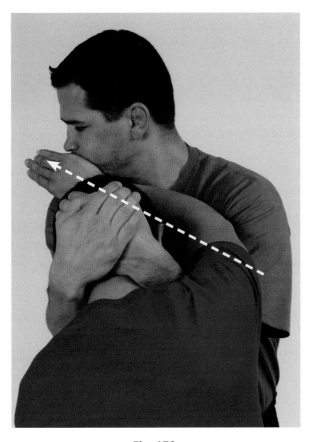

Fig. 159.

Keep contact with right hand and pummel in with left hand through inside of opponent's arms. Place left hand above opponent's neck and on back of opponent's head on round area of opponent's skull. "Cup" back of opponent's head with palm facing you.

If moving into a double head grab tie-up, continue by releasing right hand and immediately shoot right hand through inside of opponent's arms in a straight line directly past left side of opponent's head. Shoot right hand at eye-level as close to opponent as possible. Roll right shoulder forward and against right side of face for coverage. Place right hand over left hand in a palm over palm position. **Move to entire double head grab tie-up position.**

If moving into a left high-low tie-up, continue by releasing right hand and immediately move right hand to opponent's left hip. Place palm on opponent's left hipbone and relax right arm until desired motion is needed. **Move to entire left high-low tie-up position.**

You can also move into an under arm tie-up by initially shooting the left arm under opponent's right arm as high as possible under opponent's armpit. Follow by shooting right arm under opponent's left armpit and grab or clasp hands together behind opponent's back. **Do not lock fingers.** *Move to entire under arm tie-up position.*

The right cross-face can be done from an existing tie-up to switch tie-ups or gain inside dominant control.

ELBOW RAISE (LEFT)

The left elbow raise is a way to switch tie-ups or switch to a dominant inside position in the plum/clinch.

Drop level substantially by bending both knees and step forward with left leg on centerline. (Fig. 160)

Open both hands and slightly "cup" hands. Place palms under opponent's elbows and align your elbows in a direct vertical line underneath palms. Keep fingers to outside of opponent's arms.

Do not grab. (Fig. 161)

Stand and push opponent's elbows up to straighten opponent's elbows to create space.

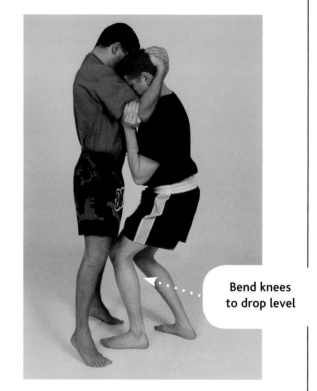

Bend knees to drop level

Fig. 160.

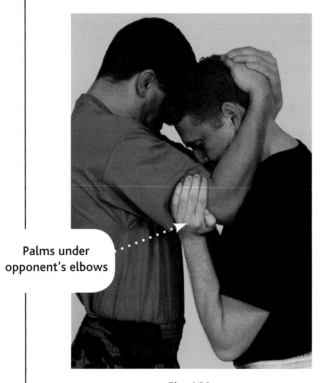

Palms under opponent's elbows

Fig. 161.

Immediately pummel in with left hand through inside of opponent's arms. Place left hand above opponent's neck and on back of opponent's head on round area of opponent's skull. "Cup" back of opponent's head with palm facing you.

If moving into a double head grab tie-up, continue by releasing right hand and immediately shoot right hand through inside of opponent's arms in a straight line directly past left side of opponent's head. Shoot right hand at eye-level as close to opponent as possible. Roll right shoulder forward and against right side of face for coverage. Place right hand over left hand in a palm over palm position. **Move to entire double head grab tie-up position.**

*If moving into a left high-low tie-up, continue by releasing right hand and immediately move right hand to opponent's left hip. Place palm on opponent's left hipbone and relax right arm until desired motion is needed. **Move to entire left high-low tie-up position.***

*You can also move into an under arm tie-up by initially shooting the left arm under opponent's right arm as high as possible under opponent's armpit. Follow by shooting right arm under opponent's left armpit and grab or clasp hands together behind opponent's back. **Do not lock fingers. Move to entire under arm tie-up position.***

The left elbow raise can be done from an existing tie-up to switch tie-ups or gain inside dominant control.

ELBOW RAISE (RIGHT)

The right elbow raise is a way to switch tie-ups or switch to a dominant inside position in the plum/clinch.

Drop level substantially by bending both knees and step forward with right leg on centerline. (Fig. 162)

Open both hands and slightly "cup" hands. Place palms under opponent's elbows and align your elbows in a direct vertical line underneath palms. Keep fingers to outside of opponent's arms.

Do not grab. (Fig. 163)

Stand and push opponent's elbows up to straighten opponent's elbows to create space.

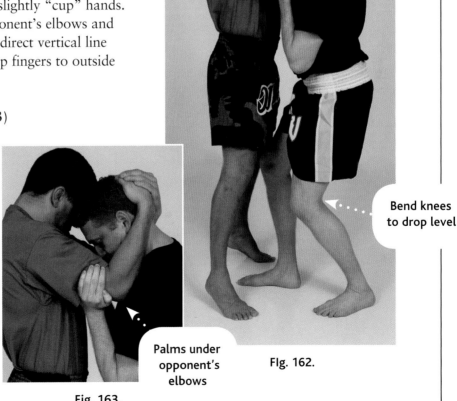

Bend knees to drop level

Palms under opponent's elbows

Fig. 162.

Fig. 163.

Immediately pummel in with right hand through inside of opponent's arms. Place right hand above opponent's neck and on back of opponent's head on round area of opponent's skull. "Cup" back of opponent's head with palm facing you.

If moving into a double head grab tie-up, continue by releasing left hand and immediately shoot left hand through inside of opponent's arms and in a straight line directly past right side of opponent's head. Shoot left hand at eye-level as close to opponent as possible. Roll left shoulder forward and against left side of face for coverage. Place left hand over right hand in a palm over palm position. **Move to entire double head grab tie-up position.**

If moving into a right high-low tie-up, continue by releasing left hand and immediately move left hand to opponent's right hip. Place palm on opponent's right hipbone and relax left arm until desired motion is needed. **Move to entire right high-low tie-up position.**

You can also move into an under arm tie-up by initially shooting the right arm under opponent's left arm as high as possible under opponent's armpit. Follow by shooting left arm under opponent's right armpit and grab or clasp hands together behind opponent's back. **Do not lock fingers.** *Move to entire under arm tie-up position.*

The right elbow raise can be done from an existing tie-up to switch tie-ups or gain inside dominant control.

ELBOW PULL (LEFT)

The left elbow pull is a way to switch tie-ups or switch to a dominant inside position in the plum/clinch.

"Cup" left hand and place left palm on outside of opponent's right elbow. Raise left elbow and align in a horizontal line with left palm. Left elbow and left palm will pull opponent's right elbow down and to the right to twist opponent's upper body and create space.

Left palm on opponent's elbow.

Fig. 164.

Do not grab. (Fig. 164-165)

Keep contact with left hand and immediately pummel in with right hand through inside of opponent's arms. Place right hand above opponent's neck and on back of opponent's head on round area of opponent's skull. "Cup" back of opponent's head with palm facing you.

Fig. 165.

If moving into a double head grab tie-up, continue by releasing left hand and immediately shoot left hand through inside of opponent's arms and in a straight line directly past right side of opponent's head. Shoot left hand at eye-level as close to opponent as possible. Roll left shoulder forward and against left side of face for coverage. Place left hand over right hand in a palm over palm position. **Move to entire double head grab tie-up position.**

If moving into a right high-low tie-up, continue by releasing left hand and immediately move left hand to opponent's right hip. Place palm on opponent's right hipbone and relax left arm until desired motion is needed. **Move to entire right high-low tie-up position.**

You can also move into an under arm tie-up by initially shooting the right arm under opponent's left arm as high as possible under opponent's armpit. Follow by shooting left arm under opponent's right armpit and grab or clasp hands together behind opponent's back. **Do not lock fingers.** *Move to entire under arm tie-up position.*

The left elbow pull can be done from an existing tie-up to switch tie-ups or gain inside dominant control.

ELBOW PULL (RIGHT)

The right elbow pull is a way to switch tie-ups or switch to a dominant inside position in the plum/clinch.

"Cup" right hand and place right palm on outside of opponent's left elbow. Raise right elbow and align in a horizontal line with right palm. Right elbow and right palm will pull opponent's left elbow down and to the left to twist opponent's upper body and create space.

Do not grab. (Fig. 166)

Fig. 166.

Keep contact with right hand and immediately pummel in with left hand through inside of opponent's arms. Place left hand above opponent's neck and on back of opponent's head on round area of opponent's skull. "Cup" back of opponent's head with palm facing you.

*If moving into a double head grab tie-up, continue by releasing right hand and immediately shoot right hand through inside of opponent's arms in a straight line directly past left side of opponent's head. Shoot right hand at eye-level as close to opponent as possible. Roll right shoulder forward and against right side of face for coverage. Place right hand over left hand in a palm over palm position. **Move to entire double head grab tie-up position.***

*If moving into a left high-low tie-up, continue by releasing right hand and immediately move right hand to opponent's left hip. Place palm on opponent's left hipbone and relax right arm until desired motion is needed. **Move to entire left high-low tie-up position.***

You can also move into an under arm tie-up by initially shooting the left arm under opponent's right arm as high as possible under opponent's armpit. Follow by shooting right arm under opponent's left armpit and grab or clasp hands together behind opponent's back. **Do not lock fingers.** *Move to entire under arm tie-up position.*

The right elbow pull can be done from an existing tie-up to switch tie-ups or gain inside dominant control.

OVER/UNDER SNAKE (LEFT)

The left over/under snake is a way to switch tie-ups or switch to a dominant inside position in the plum/clinch.

Open left hand and "cup" slightly. Move left hand from outside of opponent's right arm over opponent's right arm and continue to "snake" under opponent's left arm, creating a "wedge." The backside of your left hand will make contact underneath opponent's left forearm.

Push down with left elbow and up with back of left hand. Rotate arm counter-clockwise until arm is as vertical as possible on centerline, tilting opponent's upper body to your left while creating space. (Fig. 167)

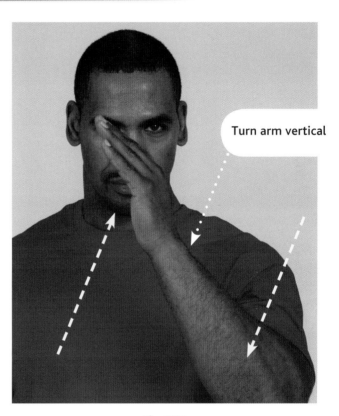

Turn arm vertical

Fig. 167.

Keep contact with left arm and pummel in with right hand through inside of opponent's arms. Place right hand above opponent's neck and on back of opponent's head on round area of opponent's skull. "Cup" back of opponent's head with palm facing you.

If moving into a double head grab tie-up, continue by releasing left arm and immediately shoot left hand through inside of opponent's arms and in a straight line directly past right side of opponent's head. Shoot left hand at eye-level as close to opponent as possible. Roll left shoulder forward and against left side of face for coverage. Place left hand over right hand in a palm over palm position. **Move to entire double head grab tie-up position.**

*If moving into a right high-low tie-up, continue by releasing left arm and immediately move left hand to opponent's right hip. Place palm on opponent's right hipbone and relax left arm until desired motion is needed. **Move to entire right high-low tie-up position.***

*You can also move into an under arm tie-up by initially shooting the right arm under opponent's left arm as high as possible under opponent's armpit. Follow by shooting left arm under opponent's right armpit and grab or clasp hands together behind opponent's back. **Do not lock fingers. Move to entire under arm tie-up position.***

The left over/under snake can be done from an existing tie-up to switch tie-ups or gain inside dominant control.

OVER/UNDER SNAKE (RIGHT)

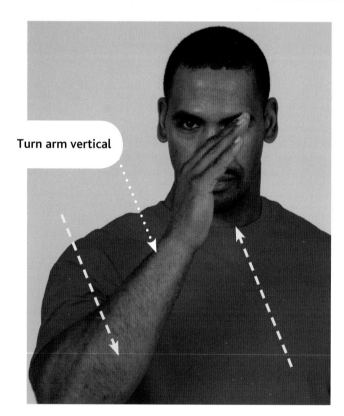

Turn arm vertical

Fig. 168.

The right over/under snake is a way to switch tie-ups or switch to a dominant inside position in the plum/clinch.

Open right hand and "cup" slightly. Move right hand from outside of opponent's left arm over opponent's left arm and continue to "snake" under opponent's right arm, creating a "wedge." The backside of your right hand will make contact underneath opponent's right forearm.

Push down with right elbow and up with back of right hand. Rotate arm clockwise until arm is as vertical as possible on centerline, tilting opponent's upper body to your right while creating space. (Fig.168)

Keep contact with right arm and pummel in with left hand through inside of opponent's arms. Place left hand above opponent's neck and on back of opponent's head on round area of opponent's skull. "Cup" back of opponent's head with palm facing you.

If moving into a double head grab tie-up, continue by releasing right arm and immediately shoot right hand through inside of opponent's arms in a straight line directly past left side of opponent's head. Shoot right hand at eye-level as close to opponent as possible. Roll right shoulder forward and against right side of face for coverage. Place right hand over left hand in a palm over palm position. **Move to entire double head grab tie-up position.**

If moving into a left high-low tie-up, continue by releasing right arm and immediately move right hand to opponent's left hip. Place palm on opponent's left hipbone and relax right arm until desired motion is needed. **Move to entire left high-low tie-up position.**

You can also move into an under arm tie-up by initially shooting the left arm under opponent's right arm as high as possible under opponent's armpit. Follow by shooting right arm under opponent's left armpit and grab or clasp hands together behind opponent's back. **Do not lock fingers.** *Move to entire under arm tie-up position.*

The right over/under snake can be done from an existing tie-up to switch tie-ups or gain inside dominant control.

PLUM/CLINCH STRIKES

SKIP KNEES #1

The skip knees #1 is a fast power technique used to strike in the plum/clinch.

From a plum/clinch tie-up, step back one full step with left leg and position left foot pointing directly toward opponent. Move left hip back to create space. Pivot right foot slightly to the left on ball of right foot to position right foot straight toward opponent. Distribute 80% of weight on right leg and 20% on left leg. Stay on balls of feet.

Strike by lifting and bending left knee while quickly thrusting it forward directly at target (mid-section of opponent). Move left hip forward. Left foot will point toes down. Raise right heel during the strike and be completely on ball of right foot.

Do not pivot. Arms will stay in existing plum/clinch tie-up position throughout technique. (Fig. 169)

After the impact, place left foot down pointing directly toward opponent in a parallel position to right foot. Simultaneously, quickly slide right foot back one full step. Move right hip back to create space. Point both feet straight toward opponent. Distribute 80% of weight on left leg and 20% on right leg. Stay on balls of feet.

Right leg is now in position to strike in the same way as previously done with left leg.

Quickly alternate strikes with right and left leg.

Stay as close to opponent as possible and only create space to allow room for your strikes.

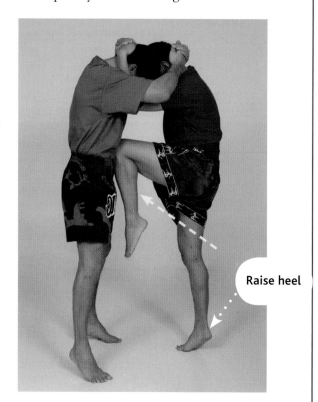

Raise heel

Fig. 169. Skip knee #1, left leg

Strikes will move in a direct line to target. Strike with kneecaps.

You can transition into skip knees #1 by getting into striking position with the right or left leg first depending on position and desired effect to opponent.

You can use your elbows to "bump" opponent away (do not release tie-up position) and immediately use your hands and arms to pull opponent into the strike for added impact and to keep opponent off balance.

The skip knees #1 also can be used as a single strike.

SKIP KNEES #2

The skip knees #2 is a power technique used to strike in the plum/clinch.

From a plum/clinch tie-up, shift 100% of weight to right leg. Swing left leg behind you and extend left leg almost completely straight behind you at waist level. Left hip will move back and completely "open up" (right hip will rotate towards opponent) to create space and allow left leg to rotate counter-clockwise to the left. Left knee and left toes will point to the left. Pivot right foot slightly to the left on ball of right foot to align left foot straight toward opponent. (Fig. 170)

Fig. 170. Skip knee #2, left leg

Strike by swinging left leg forward. Left hip will thrust forward allowing left leg to rotate clockwise to the right aligning knee straight towards target (mid-section of opponent). Bend left knee. Left foot will point toes down.

During the strike, pivot right leg to the left by pivoting on ball of right foot and raising right heel. Arms will stay in existing plum/clinch tie-up position throughout technique.

After the impact, place left foot down pointing directly toward opponent in a parallel position to the right foot. Shift 100% of weight to left leg. Swing right leg behind you and extend right leg almost completely straight behind you at waist level. Right hip will move back and completely "open up" to allow right leg to rotate clockwise to the right. Right knee and right toes will point to the right.

Right leg is now in position to strike in the same way as previously done with left leg.

Alternate strikes with right and left leg.

Stay as close to opponent as possible and only create space to allow room for your strikes.

Strikes will move in a direct line to target. Strike with kneecaps.

You can transition into skip knees #2 by getting into striking position with the right or left leg first depending on position and desired effect to opponent.

You can use your elbows to "bump" opponent away (do not release tie-up position) and immediately use your hands and arms to pull opponent into the strike for added impact and keep the opponent off balance.

The skip knees #2 also can be used as a single strike.

CURVE KNEE (LEFT)

The left curve knee is a power strike used in the plum/clinch.

From a plum/clinch tie-up, shift 100% of weight to right leg. Left hip will move back and completely "open up" (right hip will rotate towards opponent) to create space. Lift and bend left knee at waist level while moving left leg to the left. Left knee and foot will point directly to the left. Pivot right foot slightly to the left on ball of right foot to align right foot straight toward opponent. (Fig. 171)

Strike by moving inside of left knee forward and to the right directly at target (right torso of opponent). Move left hip forward. Left foot will point toes up.

Right foot will slide to the right during the strike to increase momentum.

Use arms and hands in existing plum/clinch tie-up position to pull opponent to the left into the strike for added impact and keep opponent off balance.

After the impact, place left foot down in a parallel position to right foot and return to entire plum/clinch tie-up position.

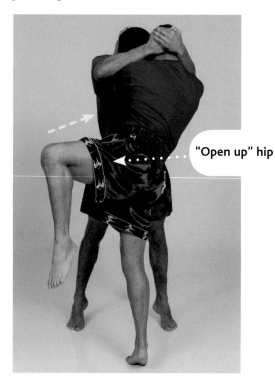

"Open up" hip

Fig. 171.

Stay as close to opponent as possible and only create space to allow room for your strike.

The strike will move from left to right.

Strike with inside of left knee.

You can also alternate between the left curve knee and the right curve knee for multiple strikes.

*You can change the left curve knee into a **left chip knee** by striking at a downward angle with the inside of the left knee and targeting opponent's upper right leg. During the strike, do not slide to the right or pull opponent to the left.*

CURVE KNEE (RIGHT)

The right curve knee is a power strike used in the plum/clinch.

From a plum/clinch tie-up, shift 100% of weight to left leg. Right hip will move back and completely "open up" (left hip will rotate towards opponent) to create space. Lift and bend right knee at waist level while moving right leg to the right. Right knee and foot will point directly to the right. Pivot left foot to the right on ball of left foot to align left foot straight toward opponent. (Fig. 172)

Strike by moving inside of right knee forward and to the left directly at target (left torso of opponent). Move right hip forward. Right foot will point toes up.

Left foot will slide to the left during the strike to increase momentum.

Use arms and hands in existing plum/clinch tie-up position to pull opponent to the right into the strike for added impact and keep opponent off balance.

After the impact, place right foot down in a parallel position to left foot shoulder length apart and return to entire plum/clinch tie-up position.

Stay as close to opponent as possible and only create space to allow room for your strike.

The strike will move from right to left.

Strike with inside of right knee.

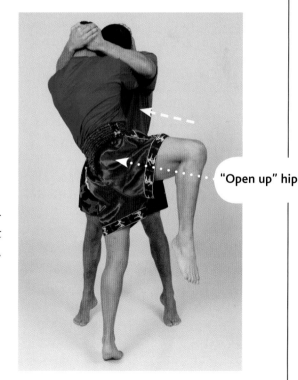

"Open up" hip

Fig. 172.

You can also alternate between the right curve knee and the left curve knee for multiple strikes.

*You can change the right curve knee into a **right chip knee** by striking at a downward angle with the inside of the left knee and targeting opponent's upper left leg. During the strike, do not slide to the right or pull opponent to the left.*

SNAP ELBOW (LEFT)

The left snap elbow is a fast snapping strike used in the plum/clinch.

From a plum/clinch tie-up, while right hand is pummeled in and "cupping" back of opponent's head, use arms to "jerk" or push opponent's head back to create space. **Do not let go** with right hand. While creating space, move left hand from plum/clinch and position left arm for a horizontal, up, or down left elbow. Immediately strike with left elbow while simultaneously using right hand to "jerk" or pull opponent's head forward into left elbow.

After the strike, return to entire plum/clinch tie-up position.

The strike can be used to rip and tear with the point of the elbow or hit with the bottom three inches of the outer forearm near the elbow. (Fig. 173)

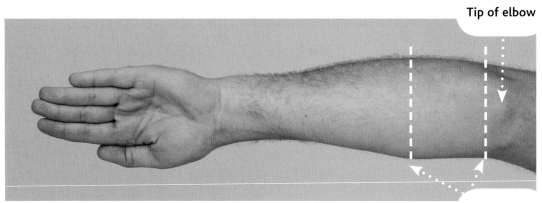

Tip of elbow

Bottom three inches

Fig. 173.

The strike will move in the desired direction of the type of left elbow used.

Stay as close to opponent as possible and only create space to allow room for your strike.

You can also use the left snap elbow to position opponent for a right elbow strike by initially positioning the left hand past the left side of opponent's head and rotate the wrist clockwise to "cup" the back of opponent's neck with the left palm. (Fig. 174)

"Cup" with left hand

Fig. 174.

Bend left elbow and pull opponent's head toward you and down against left forearm. Quickly snap left elbow up thrusting opponent's head backwards and up. Release left hand and immediately strike with a horizontal, up, or down right elbow.

After the strike, return to a plum/clinch tie-up.

SNAP ELBOW (RIGHT)

The right snap elbow is a fast snapping strike used in the plum/clinch.

From a plum/clinch tie-up, while left hand is pummeled in and "cupping" back of opponent's head, use arms to "jerk" or push opponent's head back to create space. **Do not let go** with left hand. While creating space, move right hand from plum/clinch and position right arm for a horizontal, up, or down right elbow. Immediately strike with right elbow while simultaneously using left hand to "jerk" or pull opponent's head forward into right elbow.

After the strike, return to entire plum/clinch tie-up position.

The strike can be used to rip and tear with the point of the elbow or hit with the bottom three inches of the outer forearm near the elbow. (Fig. 175)

The strike will move in the desired direction of the type of right elbow used.

Stay as close to opponent as possible and only create space to allow room for your strike.

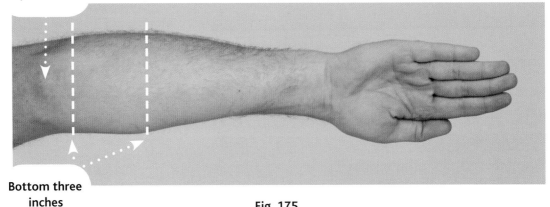

Tip of elbow

Bottom three
inches

Fig. 175.

You can also use the right snap elbow to position opponent for a left elbow strike by initially positioning the right hand past the right side of opponent's head and rotate the wrist counter-clockwise to "cup" the back of opponent's neck with the right palm. (Fig. 176)

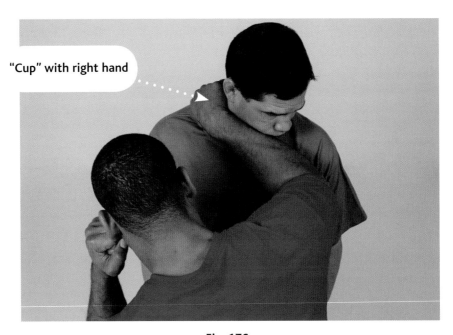

"Cup" with right hand

Fig. 176.

Bend right elbow and pull opponent's head toward you and down against right forearm. Quickly snap right elbow up thrusting opponent's head backwards and up. Release right hand and immediately strike with a horizontal, up, or down left elbow.

After the strike, return to a plum/clinch tie-up.

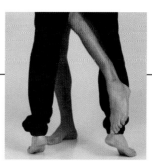

PLUM/CLINCH DEFENSES

HIP CHECK (LEFT)

HIP CHECK (RIGHT)

HIP SHIFT (LEFT)

HIP SHIFT (RIGHT)

PULL OFF BALANCE (LEFT)

PULL OFF BALANCE (RIGHT)

HEAD PULL (LEFT)

HEAD PULL (RIGHT)

LEG TIE OUTSIDE (LEFT)

LEG TIE OUTSIDE (RIGHT)

LEG TIE INSIDE (LEFT)

LEG TIE INSIDE (RIGHT)

HIP CHECK (LEFT)

The left hip check is a defense against opponent's right skip knee or right curve knee in the plum/clinch.

From plum/clinch tie-up, as you **feel** opponent's right hip move away to create space for a right knee, "cup" left hand and place on opponent's right hip. Place left palm on opponent's right hipbone. As opponent starts to strike with a right knee, thrust left hand forward pushing opponent's right hip backwards, disrupting opponent's strike and keeping opponent's right hip from moving forward. (Fig. 177)

Move left hand back to plum/clinch tie-up position.

If you are in a right high-low tie-up, your left hand is already in position to disrupt opponent's right knee.

The left hip check is used to block the forward progress of opponent's right hip, disrupting opponent's right knee.

Fig. 177. Block hip

HIP CHECK (RIGHT)

The right hip check is a defense against opponent's left skip knee or left curve knee in the plum/clinch.

From plum/clinch tie-up, as you **feel** opponent's left hip move away to create space for a left knee, "cup" right hand and place on opponent's left hip. Place right palm on opponent's left hipbone. As opponent starts to strike with a left knee, thrust right hand forward pushing opponent's left hip backwards, disrupting opponent's strike and keeping opponent's left hip from moving forward. (Fig. 178)

Move right hand back to plum/clinch tie-up position.

If you are in a left high-low tie-up, your right hand is already in position to disrupt opponent's left knee.

The right hip check is used to block the forward progress of opponent's left hip, disrupting opponent's left knee.

Fig. 178. Block hip

HIP SHIFT (LEFT)

The left hip shift is a defense against opponent's right skip knee or right curve knee in the plum/clinch.

From plum/clinch tie-up, as you **feel** opponent's right hip move away to create space for a right knee and opponent starts to strike with the right knee, rotate left hip to the right toward opponent and thrust left hip forward into opponent's right hip, pushing opponent's right hip backwards to disrupt opponent's strike.

Move left hip back to plum/clinch tie-up position.

The left hip shift is used to block the forward progress of opponent's right hip, disrupting opponent's right knee.

HIP SHIFT (RIGHT)

The right hip shift is a defense against opponent's left skip knee or left curve knee in the plum/clinch.

From plum/clinch tie-up, as you **feel** opponent's left hip move away to create space for a left knee and opponent starts to strike with the left knee, rotate right hip to the left toward opponent and thrust right hip forward into opponent's left hip, pushing opponent's left hip backwards to disrupt opponent's strike.

Move right hip back to plum/clinch tie-up position.

The right hip shift is used to block the forward progress of opponent's left hip, disrupting opponent's left knee.

PULL OFF BALANCE (LEFT)

The left pull off balance is a technique used to disrupt opponent's strike, move opponent into your strike, and/or reposition opponent to keep opponent off balance in the plum/clinch.

From any plum/clinch tie-up position, **twist** opponent's upper body to the left (lead with opponent's head) and "jerk" or pull opponent to the left with hands and arms. Use legs to push or pull opponent to the left. Your upper body will follow opponent to the left to increase momentum.

Maintain arm tie-up position throughout technique.

Stay as close to opponent as possible and only create space to allow room for your strike or to reposition opponent from pull off balance.

Use the left pull off balance to disrupt opponent's strike. During opponent's strike, pull off balance to the left.

Use the left pull off balance to move opponent into your left strike and increase the impact.

Use the left pull off balance to keep opponent off balance so opponent cannot strike, and/or position opponent for your strike.

PULL OFF BALANCE (RIGHT)

The right pull off balance is a technique used to disrupt opponent's strike, move opponent into your strike, and/or reposition opponent to keep opponent off balance in the plum/clinch.

From any plum/clinch tie-up position, **twist** opponent's upper body to the right (lead with opponent's head) and "jerk" or pull opponent to the right with hands and arms. Use legs to push or pull opponent to the right. Your upper body will follow opponent to the right to increase momentum.

Maintain arm tie-up position throughout technique.

Stay as close to opponent as possible and only create space to allow room for your strike or to reposition opponent from pull off balance.

Use the right pull off balance to disrupt opponent's strike. During opponent's strike, pull off balance to the right.

Use the right pull off balance to move opponent into your right strike and increase the impact.

Use the right pull off balance to keep opponent off balance so opponent cannot strike, and/or position opponent for your strike.

HEAD PULL (LEFT)

The left head pull is a defense against opponent's right skip knee or right curve knee in the plum/clinch.

From plum/clinch tie-up, as you **feel** opponent's right hip move away to create space for a right skip or right curve knee and opponent starts to strike with the right knee, pull opponent's head down toward your abdomen while taking a full step back with left leg to draw opponent toward you. Keep arms and hands in the tie-up position throughout the head pull technique to maintain control and keep opponent moving forward and close to you. (Fig. 179)

Pull head down

Step back with left leg and draw opponent toward you

Fig. 179.

The left head pull disrupts opponent's right skip or right curve knee by pulling opponent forward off balance forcing opponent's kneeing leg to be quickly placed on the ground for balance.

After the head pull, immediately follow-up with a strike or quickly close the distance and return to original plum/clinch tie-up.

If you pull opponent's head below your shoulder level during the head pull, immediately follow-up with a left knee strike.

HEAD PULL (RIGHT)

The right head pull is a defense against opponent's left skip knee or left curve knee in the plum/clinch.

From plum/clinch tie-up: as you **feel** opponent's left hip move away to create space for a left skip or left curve knee and opponent starts to strike with the left knee, pull opponent's head down toward your abdomen while taking a full step back with right leg to draw opponent toward you. Keep arms and hands in the tie-up position throughout the head pull technique to maintain control and keep opponent moving forward and close to you. (Fig. 180)

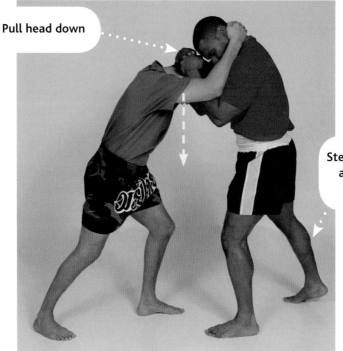

Pull head down

Step back with right leg and draw opponent toward you

Fig. 180.

The right head pull disrupts opponent's left skip or left curve knee by pulling opponent forward off balance forcing opponent's kneeing leg to be quickly placed on the ground for balance.

After the head pull, immediately follow-up with a strike or quickly close the distance and return to original plum/clinch tie-up.

If you pull opponent's head below your shoulder level during the head pull, immediately follow-up with a right knee strike.

LEG TIE OUTSIDE (LEFT)

The left leg tie outside is a technique used to disrupt opponent's strike, move opponent off balance, throw, and/or sweep opponent's left leg in the plum/clinch.

From any plum/clinch tie-up position, shift 100% of weight to right leg and move left leg to the outside and behind opponent's right leg (i.e., "hook" the leg). Thrust left leg toward you and/or to the right, pulling or "jerking" opponent's right leg.

Maintain balance with right leg. (Fig. 181)

Stay as close to opponent as possible and only create space to allow room for your strike or for repositioning of opponent from the left leg tie.

Use the left leg tie outside to disrupt opponent's left knee by "sweeping" opponent's right base leg.

Use the left leg tie outside to hook opponent's right leg to stop opponent's right knee.

Use the left leg tie outside to keep opponent off balance so opponent cannot strike, and/or position opponent for your strike. It also can be used in combination with the pull off balance to throw, sweep or keep opponent off balance.

Fig. 181.

After the desired effect, place left leg back to plum/clinch tie-up position.

LEG TIE OUTSIDE (RIGHT)

The right leg tie outside is a technique used to disrupt opponent's strike, move opponent off balance, throw, and/or sweep opponent's left leg in the plum/clinch.

From any plum/clinch tie-up position, shift 100% of weight to left leg and move right leg to the outside and behind opponent's left leg (i.e., "hook" the leg). Thrust right leg toward you and/or to the left, pulling or "jerking" opponent's left leg.

Maintain balance with left leg. (Fig. 182)

Fig. 182.

Stay as close to opponent as possible and only create space to allow room for your strike or for repositioning of opponent from the right leg tie.

Use the right leg tie outside to disrupt opponent's right knee by "sweeping" opponent's left base leg.

Use the right leg tie outside to hook opponent's left leg to stop opponent's left knee.

*Use the right leg tie outside to keep opponent off balance so opponent cannot strike, and/or position opponent for your strike. **It also can be used in combination with the pull off balance to throw, sweep or keep opponent off balance.***

After the desired effect, place right leg back to plum/clinch tie-up position.

LEG TIE INSIDE (LEFT)

The left leg tie inside is a technique used to disrupt opponent's strike, move opponent off balance, throw, and/or sweep opponent's left leg in the plum/clinch.

From any plum/clinch tie-up position, shift 100% of weight to right leg and move left leg to the inside and behind opponent's right leg (i.e., "hook" the leg). Thrust left leg toward you and/or to the left, pulling or "jerking" opponent's right leg.

Maintain balance with right leg. (Fig. 183)

Stay as close to opponent as possible and only create space to allow room for your strike or for repositioning of opponent from the left leg tie.

Use the left leg tie inside to disrupt opponent's left knee by "sweeping" opponent's right base leg.

Use the left leg tie inside to hook opponent's right leg to stop opponent's right knee.

*Use the left leg tie inside to keep opponent off balance so opponent cannot strike, and/or position opponent for your strike. **It also can be used in combination with the pull off balance to throw, sweep or keep opponent off balance.***

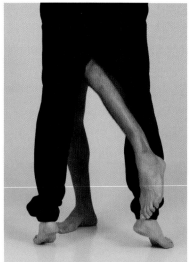

Fig. 183.

After the desired effect, place left leg back to plum/clinch tie-up position.

LEG TIE INSIDE (RIGHT)

The right leg tie inside is a technique used to disrupt opponent's strike, move opponent off balance, throw, and/or sweep opponent's left leg in the plum/clinch.

From any plum/clinch tie-up position, shift 100% of weight to left leg and move right leg to the inside and behind opponent's left leg (i.e., "hook" the leg). Thrust right leg toward you and/or to the right, pulling or "jerking" opponent's left leg.

Maintain balance with left leg. (Fig. 184)

Stay as close to opponent as possible and only create space to allow room for your strike or for repositioning of opponent from the right leg tie.

Use the right leg tie inside to disrupt opponent's right knee by "sweeping" opponent's left base leg.

Use the right leg tie inside to hook opponent's left leg to stop opponent's left knee.

*Use the right leg tie inside to keep opponent off balance so opponent cannot strike, and/or position opponent for your strike. **It also can be used in combination with the pull off balance to throw, sweep or keep opponent off balance.***

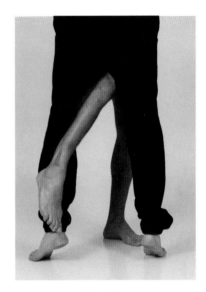

Fig. 184.

After the desired effect, place right leg back to plum/clinch tie-up position.

 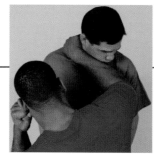 

PLUM/CLINCH THROWS

THROW (LEFT)

The left throw is a technique used to break a plum/clinch tie-up, throw opponent off balance, and/or position opponent for an attack.

From any plum/clinch tie-up position, step right leg one full step forward and slightly to the right. Pivot to the left on balls of both feet and rotate your entire body to the left. During the pivot, use hands and arms to **twist** opponent's upper body to the left (lead with opponent's head) and push/throw-out opponent to the left. Release all contact with opponent.

From a double head grab tie-up, use both elbows to "bump" opponent's upper body up and backwards during the release.

From a left or right high-low tie-up, use elbow of the arm in the high position to "bump" opponent's upper body up and backwards during the release.

Stay as close to opponent as possible until the throw-out.

After the left throw, return to Muay Thai stance to follow-up or defend.

THROW (RIGHT)

The right throw is a technique used to break a plum/clinch tie-up, throw opponent off balance, and/or position opponent for an attack.

From any plum/clinch tie-up position, step left leg one full step forward and slightly to the left. Pivot to the right on balls of both feet and rotate your entire body to the right. During the pivot, use hands and arms to **twist** opponent's upper body to the right (lead with opponent's head) and push/throw-out opponent to the right. Release all contact with opponent.

From a double head grab tie-up, use both elbows to "bump" opponent's upper body up and backwards during the release.

From a left or right high-low tie-up, use elbow of the arm in the high position to "bump" opponent's upper body up and backwards during the release.

Stay as close to opponent as possible until the throw-out.

After the left throw, return to Muay Thai stance to follow-up or defend.

PERSONAL ATTACK RANGE

The personal attack range is the area around you broken down into three areas: close range, medium range, and long range. (Fig. 185)

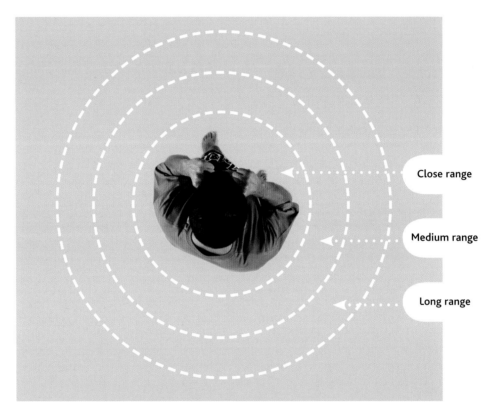

Fig. 185. Top View

You are the nucleus contained within the three circle areas. As you move, the areas move with you, maintaining the same distance.

Learn what techniques you can perform in each range area to accomplish a successful attack.

Learn to recognize when an opponent enters each range so that you can respond accordingly.

The distance of the ranges will vary for each individual depending on size and reach.

RANGE TABLE

The range table shows what strikes are most effective in the different ranges (distance) between you and your opponent.

RANGE TABLE

STRIKE	RANGE		
Jab		Medium	Long
Cross		Medium	Long
Hook	Close	Medium	
Uppercut	Close		
Elbow	Close		
Spinning Back-Fist		Medium	Long
Spinning Back-Elbow	Close	Medium	
Jump Fly Cross			Long
Jump Fly Elbow			Long
Round Kick		Medium	Long
Long Foot Jab		Medium	Long
Short Foot Jab		Medium	
Long Knee		Medium	
Cut Kick		Medium	Long
Straight Knee	Close		
Jump Fly Knee			Long
Angle Kick		Medium	
Plum/Clinch Strike	Close		

EQUIPMENT

There are two types of basic equipment used for training in Muay Thai: protective equipment and training equipment.

PROTECTIVE EQUIPMENT

Always wear the proper protective equipment that coincides with the specific training you will perform.

Thai boxing shorts or loose clothing that allows easy movement.
Mouth Guard
Cup/Groin Protector (for males and should be worn for all training)
Heavy Gloves (for striking partner or equipment)
Shin Guards (for striking partner)
Bag Gloves (for striking equipment only)
Headgear (optional)
Wrist Wraps (optional)
Boxing or wrestling Shoes (optional)

Add additional protective equipment as needed to maintain a safe environment for all participants.

TRAINING EQUIPMENT

Always learn the proper way to use the equipment before training.

Thai Pads
Focus Mitts
Heavy bag

You can add additional training equipment to enhance your training as needed. (e.g., belly pad, jump rope, speed bag)

FOCUS MITTS

USING FOCUS MITTS

Focus mitts are used with a trainer/partner and allow one to practice using upper body strikes with speed and precision.

There are different styles and construction of focus mitts depending on the manufacturer but all maintain the basic functionality. (Fig. 186)

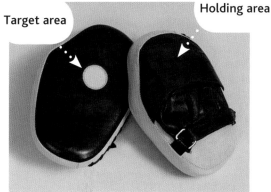

Target area **Holding area** **Palm flush**

Fig. 186.   Fig. 187.

To hold a focus mitt, secure your hand with your palm facing against the holding area of the focus mitt.

Keep palm flush against focus mitt. (Fig. 187)

The focus mitt holder will stay relaxed and maintain proper Muay Thai stance and movement.

Transition is smooth and fluid from one holding position to another.

Hold focus mitt still for the strike, then tap the strike during impact to give slight resistance.

Do not reach.

Do not hold a focus mitt directly in front of your face.

HOLDING FOCUS MITTS FOR UPPER BODY STRIKES

When holding for a single upper body strike with one focus mitt, place the other focus mitt across your chest or abdomen with striking area hidden from view.

Fig. 188.

Fig. 189.

JAB AND/OR CROSS
The holding position can be used for the left or right side by using the corresponding focus mitt.

Depending on which side the focus mitt is held, the jab or cross may strike across centerline. (Fig. 188)

HOOK
The holding position can be used for the left or right side by using the corresponding focus mitt. (Fig. 189)

UPPERCUT
The holding position can be used for the left or right side by using the corresponding focus mitt.

Hold the focus mitt horizontal and approximately three inches below chin. (Fig. 190)

Fig. 190.

LOW JAB AND/OR LOW CROSS

The holding position can be used for the left or right side by using the corresponding focus mitt. (Fig. 191)

Fig. 191.

LOW HOOK

The holding position can be used for the left or right side by using the corresponding focus mitt.

Hold the focus mitt horizontal with the top of the focus mitt toward the striker. (Fig. 192)

Fig. 192.

COMBINATION HOLDING

Use both focus mitts and combine holds for multiple upper body strikes (e.g., cross—low hook) (Fig. 193)

*Some training drills require you to strike while holding focus mitts. Use the padded surface of the focus mitts and strike **lightly** using proper Muay Thai techniques.*

Fig. 193.

THAI PADS

USING THAI PADS

Thai pads are used with a trainer/partner and allow one to practice using upper body strikes and/or lower body strikes with full power.

There are different styles and construction of Thai pads depending on the manufacturer but all maintain the basic functionality. (Fig. 194)

To hold a Thai pad, secure your arm with the inner forearm and palm facing the holding area of the Thai pad. Grab the handle in a fist position.

Keep fingers and thumb tight at all times. (Fig. 195)

The Thai pad holder will use a mouth guard to prevent jarring during impact.

The Thai pad holder will stay relaxed and maintain proper Muay Thai stance and movement.

Transition is smooth and fluid from one holding position to another.

Hold Thai pad still for the strike.

Do not reach.

Do not hold a Thai pad directly in front of your face.

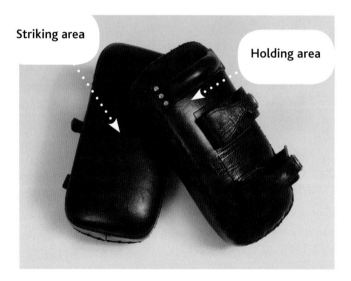

Striking area

Holding area

Fig. 194.

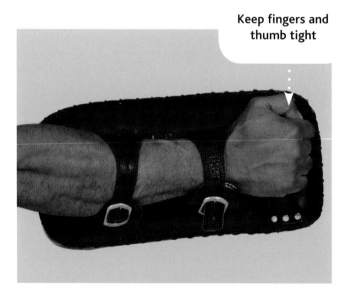

Keep fingers and thumb tight

Fig. 195.

HOLDING THAI PADS FOR UPPER BODY STRIKES

When holding for a single upper body strike with one Thai pad, place the other Thai pad across your chest or abdomen with the striking area hidden from view.

JAB AND/OR CROSS

The holding position can be used for the left or right side by using the corresponding Thai pad.

Depending on which side the Thai pad is held, the jab or cross may strike across centerline. (Fig. 196)

Fig. 196.

Fig. 197.

HOOK

The holding position can be used for the left or right side by using the corresponding Thai pad. (Fig. 197)

UPPERCUT

The holding position can be used for the left or right side by using the corresponding Thai pad.

Hold the Thai pad horizontal and approximately three inches below chin. (Fig. 198)

Fig. 198.

LOW JAB AND/OR LOW CROSS

The holding position can be used for the left or right side by using the corresponding Thai pad. (Fig. 199)

Fig. 199.

LOW HOOK

The holding position can be used for the left or right side by using the corresponding Thai pad.

Hold the Thai pad horizontal with the top of the Thai pad toward the striker. (Fig. 200)

Fig. 200.

HORIZONTAL ELBOW

The holding position can be used for the left or right side by using the corresponding Thai pad.

Hold the Thai pad across centerline and angle the striking area of the Thai pad toward the strike. (Fig. 201)

Fig. 201.

DOWN ELBOW

The holding position can be used for the left or right side by using the corresponding Thai pad.

Hold the Thai pad across centerline and angle the striking area of the Thai pad toward the strike. (Fig. 202)

Fig. 202.

UP ELBOW

The holding position can be used for the left or right side by using the corresponding Thai pad.

Hold the Thai pad across centerline and angle the striking area of the Thai pad toward the strike. (Fig. 203)

Fig. 203.

COMBINATION HOLDING

Use both Thai pads and combine holds for multiple upper body strikes (e.g., jab—cross—hook) (Fig. 204)

Fig. 204.

HOLDING THAI PADS FOR LOWER BODY STRIKES

Fig. 205.

ROUND KICK
The holding position can be used for the left or right side.

Hold the Thai pads close and tight against your body.

The striker's shin should impact the striking area of both Thai pads equally. (Fig. 205)

Fig. 206.

ANGLE KICK
The holding position can be used for the left or right side.

Hold the Thai pads to the side and on a slight diagonal.

Hold the Thai pads close and tight against your body.

The striker's shin should impact the striking area of both Thai pads equally. (Fig. 206)

KNEE, FOOT JAB, AND/OR PLUM/CLINCH SKIP KNEE ("T" HOLD)
The holding position can be used for the left or right side.

Hold the Thai pads on a slight forward diagonal in front of your abdomen and "crunch" your midsection.

Hold the Thai pads close and tight against your body.

The striker will only strike the front horizontal Thai pad. (Fig. 207)

*Some training drills require you to strike while holding Thai pads. Use the padded surface of the Thai pads and strike **lightly** using proper Muay Thai techniques.*

"Crunch" midsection

Fig. 207.

TRAINING DRILLS

Training drills are done in multiple 3-minute rounds with a 30-second rest between rounds.

SHADOW BOXING

Use all the techniques you have learned against an imaginary opponent. Incorporate strikes, defense, combinations, and movement. Shadow boxing can be done slowly to work on proper technique and execution, or fast to work on fluidity and endurance. Shadow boxing also can be used as a warm-up.

HEAVY BAG DRILL

Strike the heavy bag with full power throughout the rounds. Pay attention to positioning, distance, and adjustment to the resistance from the heavy bag.

FOCUS MITT DRILL (UPPER BODY)

The focus mitt drill is done with a trainer/partner equipped with focus mitts. The trainer will strike **lightly** at random with the focus mitts and dictate movement, frequently stopping movement, positioning focus mitts, and calling out a number of strikes. Stay in striking range of the trainer and defend all of the trainer's strikes. Once the trainer calls a number, strike the focus mitts with the according number of strikes. Your upper body striking techniques will be determined by the positioning of the trainer's focus mitts.

THAI PAD DRILL (UPPER BODY AND/OR LOWER BODY)

The Thai pad drill is done with a trainer/partner equipped with a pair of Thai pads. The trainer will strike **lightly** at random with the Thai pads and dictate movement, frequently stopping movement, positioning Thai pads, and calling out a number of strikes. Stay in striking range of the trainer and defend all of the trainer's strikes. Once the trainer calls a number, strike the Thai pads with the according number of strikes. Your striking techniques will be determined by the positioning of the trainer's Thai pads.

DEFENSE DRILL

The defense drill is done with a partner. Both participants should be equipped with a mouth guard and heavy gloves. From Muay Thai stance, position your back as close to a wall as possible so you cannot retreat. Your partner will stand in front and in close range and continually strike with **light** contact. Defend all strikes. The drill can be done for upper and lower body defense.

TIME SPARRING

Time sparring is done with a partner. Both participants should be equipped with a mouth guard, heavy gloves, cup/groin protector (for males), shin pads, and headgear (optional). Spar making **light** contact. Allow each participant to execute combinations and counters. Defend attacks and follow-up. Keep a steady flow throughout. Start at a slow speed and increase the speed as participants feel comfortable.

PLUM/CLINCH TIE-UP DRILL

The plum/clinch tie-up drill is done with a partner. Both participants should be equipped with a mouth guard and cup/groin protector (for males). Start from the plum/clinch. Allow each participant to gain dominant inside control and alternate. Use all plum/clinch tie-ups and plum/clinch tie-up defenses. Keep a steady flow throughout. Start at a slow speed and increase the speed as participants feel comfortable.

PLUM/CLINCH SPARRING

Plum/clinch sparring is done with a partner. Both participants should be equipped with a mouth guard and cup/groin protector (for males). Start from the plum/clinch. Each participant will try to gain inside dominant control. You can only strike **lightly** with the curve knee. **Do not use any other strikes.** Use all plum/clinch tie-ups, plum/clinch tie-up defenses, plum/clinch throws, and plum/clinch defenses.

ENDURANCE DRILLS

Endurance drills are used to build up your cardio-vascular endurance by repeating a series of techniques aggressively throughout the rounds.

Endurance drills are done in multiple 3-minute rounds with a 30-second rest between rounds. The drills are done with a trainer/partner equipped with a pair of Thai pads. All strikes are done to the pads. Continually repeat the drill throughout the rounds.

ENDURANCE DRILL #1

JAB—CROSS—RIGHT ROUND KICK.

ENDURANCE DRILL #2

JAB—CROSS—LEFT HOOK—CROSS—LEFT ROUND KICK—RIGHT ROUND KICK.

ENDURANCE DRILL #3

RIGHT LONG KNEE—RIGHT ROUND KICK—LEFT LONG KNEE—LEFT ROUND KICK.

ENDURANCE DRILL #4

DOUBLE RIGHT ROUND KICK—DOUBLE LEFT ROUND KICK.

COMBINATION DRILLS

Combination drills are designed to teach you how to combine techniques and move fluidly from one to another, developing a rhythm.

The combination drills are done with a trainer/partner equipped with a pair of Thai pads. All strikes are done to the Thai pads unless noted. Combination drills may be done in multiple 3-minute rounds with a 30-second rest between rounds by continually repeating the combination throughout the rounds. In the combinations listed below, the pad holder (trainer/partner) portion is highlighted in **red bold**.

*Combinations #3, #4, #5, #6, #9, #10, #11, and #13 require you to kick the trainer/partner. When kicking the trainer/partner use **light** contact with a slight push at impact to feel the resistance.*

*Combination #11 can be done for the curve knees at full power with a trainer/partner wearing a belly pad (a protective device worn to protect the ribs and abdomen area), otherwise use **light** contact for the curve knees.*

COMBINATION #1

JAB—CROSS—RIGHT ROUND KICK TO LEG—LEAD LEG SHIELD—RIGHT ROUND KICK—LEFT ROUND KICK TO LEG—CROSS SHIELD—LEFT ROUND KICK.

COMBINATION #2

JAB—RIGHT PARRY—CROSS—LEFT PARRY—LEFT HOOK—RIGHT COVER HIGH—CROSS—LEFT COVER HIGH—CROSS—LEFT ROUND KICK—LEFT HOOK—RIGHT ROUND KICK—RIGHT ROUND KICK—RETREAT AND ADVANCE.

COMBINATION #3

JAB—RIGHT PARRY—LOW CROSS—LEFT COVER LOW INSIDE—CROSS— LOW LEFT HOOK—LEFT HOOK—SHORT FOOT JAB—LONG FOOT JAB— PARRY FOOT JAB INSIDE (LEFT)—RIGHT ROUND KICK TO TRAINER'S LEG—LEFT ROUND KICK.

COMBINATION #4

LOW JAB—JAB—CROSS—LOW LEFT HOOK—RIGHT COVER LOW OUTSIDE—LOW LEFT HOOK—CROSS—LEFT ROUND KICK—RIGHT ROUND KICK MID-LEVEL—SWEEP/PARRY ROUND KICK (RIGHT)—LEFT ROUND KICK TO TRAINER'S LEG—RIGHT ROUND KICK.

COMBINATION #5

JAB—RIGHT CUP/CATCH—CROSS—LEFT SLIP—LEFT UPPERCUT CROSS—RIGHT ROUND KICK—LEFT CUT KICK TO TRAINER—RIGHT LONG KNEE—RIGHT ROUND KICK.

COMBINATION #6

RIGHT LONG KNEE—OUTSIDE KNEE PARRY (LEFT)—LEFT ROUND KICK—RIGHT CUT KICK TO TRAINER—JAB—RIGHT UPPERCUT—LOW LEFT HOOK—LEFT HOOK—RIGHT ROUND KICK—LEFT ROUND KICK.

COMBINATION #7

JAB—CROSS—LEFT HOOK—CROSS—LEFT HOOK—BOB & WEAVE (RIGHT)—CROSS—LEFT HOOK—CROSS—BOB & WEAVE (LEFT)—LEFT HOOK—CROSS—CROSS—STRAIGHT KNEE #1—LEFT HORIZONTAL ELBOW—RIGHT HORIZONTAL ELBOW.

COMBINATION #8

RIGHT ROUND KICK—LONG FOOT JAB—CROSS—STRAIGHT KNEE #2— PUMMEL TO DOUBLE HEAD GRAB—(4) SKIP KNEES #1—THROW LEFT—RIGHT ROUND KICK—JAB—RIGHT PARRY—CROSS—LEFT PARRY—PUMMEL TO DOUBLE HEAD GRAB—(4) SKIP KNEES #2—THROW LEFT—RIGHT ROUND KICK.

COMBINATION #9

JAB—CROSS—LEFT HOOK—CROSS—CROSS—LEFT SHOULDER STOP—RIGHT DOWN ELBOW—LEFT UP ELBOW—RIGHT LONG KNEE—RIGHT ROUND KICK—RIGHT ROUND KICK—RIGHT ANGLE EVADE KICK TO TRAINER.

COMBINATION #10

RIGHT ROUND KICK—RIGHT ANGLE EVADE KICK TO TRAINER—LONG FOOT JAB—CROSS—STRAIGHT KNEE #2—LEFT DOWN ELBOW—RIGHT DOWN ELBOW—PUMMEL TO DOUBLE HEAD GRAB—(4) SKIP KNEES #2—THROW LEFT—DOUBLE RIGHT ROUND KICK.

COMBINATION #11

JAB—CROSS—LEFT HORIZONTAL ELBOW—RIGHT SPINNING BACK-ELBOW—RIGHT HORIZONTAL ELBOW—LEFT ELBOW JAM—PUMMEL TO LEFT HIGH-LOW TIE-UP—(4) ALTERNATING CURVE KNEES TO TRAINER—THROW LEFT—RIGHT ROUND KICK MID-LEVEL—LEFT CATCH KICK—LEFT CUT KICK TO TRAINER.

COMBINATION #12

RIGHT ROUND KICK MID-LEVEL—LEFT CATCH KICK—RIGHT LONG KNEE—LEFT HOOK—CROSS—LEFT ROUND KICK—RIGHT DOWN ELBOW—LEFT SPINNING BACK-ELBOW—LEFT HORIZONTAL ELBOW—RIGHT ELBOW JAM—PUMMEL TO DOUBLE HEAD GRAB—(2) SKIP KNEES #1—THROW LEFT—DOUBLE RIGHT ROUND KICK.

COMBINATION #13

RIGHT ROUND KICK—RIGHT ANGLE EVADE KICK TO TRAINER—RIGHT JUMP FLY KNEE—CROSS—STRAIGHT KNEE #2—LEFT DOWN ELBOW—RIGHT DOWN ELBOW—PUMMEL TO DOUBLE HEAD GRAB—(4) SKIP KNEES #2—THROW LEFT—RIGHT JUMP FLY ELBOW.

COMBINATION #14

RIGHT ROUND KICK—LONG FOOT JAB—CROSS—STRAIGHT KNEE #2—LEFT PUSH—RIGHT JUMP FLY ELBOW—LEFT HOOK—RIGHT ROUND KICK—RIGHT JUMP FLY KNEE—DOUBLE LEFT ROUND KICK.

COMBINATION #15

JAB—CROSS—LEFT HOOK—CROSS—HIGH LEFT HOOK—BOB & WEAVE (RIGHT)—CROSS—LEFT HOOK—HIGH RIGHT HOOK—BOB & WEAVE (LEFT)—LEFT HOOK—CROSS—LOW LEFT HOOK—RIGHT COVER LOW OUTSIDE—RIGHT UPPERCUT—LEFT HOOK—CROSS—LOW RIGHT HOOK—LEFT COVER LOW OUTSIDE—LEFT UPPERCUT—CROSS—LEFT HOOK.

SPECIFIC PROBLEM AREA TRAINING TIPS

KEEPING CHIN DOWN

Place a table tennis (ping pong) ball under chin and tuck chin to hold it in place while shadow boxing. The drill also can be done using a larger tennis ball. (Fig. 208)

MAINTAINING HAND POSITION

Place a towel around neck and grab both ends of the towel with hands at eye-level, a fist's width apart, and a fist's width from face. Maintain position while practicing movement. (Fig. 209)

Fig. 208. Ping pong ball

MAINTAINING LEGS SHOULDER-WIDTH APART AFTER MOVEMENT

Tie one end of a piece of elastic rope, cord, or band to left ankle and the other end to right ankle. Tie the rope so the length of the rope is approximately 2 inches longer than your shoulder-width. Practice movement and upper body strikes while the rope is attached. (Fig. 210)

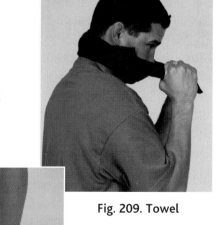

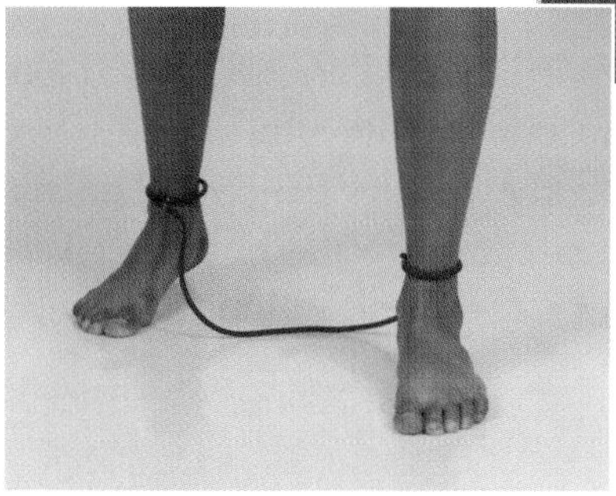

Fig. 209. Towel

Fig. 210. Elastic rubber cord

ABOUT THE AUTHOR

Joe E. Harvey is an experienced martial artist with close to 20 years of active training and teaching. Fascinated by the martial arts early on, Joe began official training at the age of ten in Youngstown, Ohio, where he was born. Joe holds a black belt from training in Muay Thai, Filipino Martial Arts, and Jeet Kune Do Concepts from Patrick Tray (see Foreword) at the Trident Academy of Martial Arts, Woodbridge, Virginia. He also holds a second degree black belt in Taekwondo from Kang Rhee (instructor to Elvis Presley and Bill "Superfoot" Wallace), Memphis, Tennessee. He received his first degree black belt from the American Taekwondo Association (ATA) (founded by the late Hueng Ung Lee), Austintown, Ohio. Joe has trained in several other martial arts and organizations such as Ji Do Kwan, Wu-Shu Kung-Fu, and Jhoon Rhee Taekwondo. He also had the privilege of training with martial arts legend, Dan Inosanto.

Joe has a wide range of martial arts knowledge and experiences from teaching and training with numerous martial artists and their different instructional styles. He has developed his skills to become an experienced technician. He studies each Art with great depth, paying close attention to the finer details that are often overlooked. With this background, Joe gives a fresh and unique approach to writing a martial art book.